WOLSEY LODGES

WELCOME

For over 30 years Wolsey Lodges have been welcoming guests into their homes.
Arriving as strangers, many guests leave as friends. Our reputation for hospitality
in some of the finest homes to be found has meant our circle of friends has grown and grown.

We welcome you to turn the page and discover Wolsey Lodges for yourself.

relax • explore • indulge • experience • enjoy

Many reasons to stay and no reason to leave

Romantic break away; family holiday; birthday celebrations; anniversary surprise; a base for for touring the area; business trip – there are many reasons why our guests choose Wolsey Lodges.

Whatever your reason for staying in a Wolsey Lodge you will find a warm welcome awaits you and sets the theme for your whole stay.

However you decide to spend your time, your Wolsey Lodge hosts will do all they can to make a world of difference to the overall enjoyment of the place you stay. And, if you are celebrating a special occasion, make sure you inform your host when you book so that you can arrange with them those extra touches to make your stay truly memorable.

Arrive and know you may not wish to leave.

GREAT EXPECTATIONS

We understand what makes a good bed and breakfast become an exceptional bed and breakfast and it all comes down to experience. We expect great things of all of our Lodges because they expect it of themselves. To each and every one of our hosts, the service they offer is a way of life and not just a way of working.

Our hosts open their homes to you and unreservedly commit themselves to making it your home also - ensuring that you relax and enjoy your time with them from the moment you arrive.

Quietly comfortable, lavishly luxurious, invariably elegant and filled to the brim with the homely touches that our hosts know, from experience, make all the difference in the world to their guests - sumptuous towels in the bathrooms, beds made up with the finest linen, books, games and music to entertain.

You will find serenity in summer, warmth in winter, delicious home-cooked food, dinner party atmospheres if you dine in the evening, blissful bedrooms, pristine bathrooms, a comfortable sitting room and peaceful gardens to arouse your senses.

Our standards are exacting as we have a lot to live up to.

Our own team of inspectors personally visit each and every Lodge to ensure they continue to offer everything our guests expect.

Many of our Lodges also invite VisitBritain and/or AA assessors to visit them and endorse our own inspector's exacting standards. These Lodges have been awarded four or five stars and some have silver and gold awards as well.

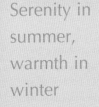

Serenity in summer, warmth in winter

From top: Molesworth Manor , Cornwall (Wolsey Lodge); Skirling House, Lanarkshire (Wolsey Lodge); Hrempis Farm, Leicestershire (Wolsey Lodge); Pentillie Castle, Cornwall (Wolsey Lodge)

iii

FIRST IMPRESSIONS

Every one of our Wolsey Lodges is a unique private home and the very nature of this uniqueness, some may call it quirkiness, is what our guests have come to expect, and indeed return to, so often.

We want you to be happy with us from the moment you first make contact and so, to make life a little easier, we have compiled the following pages of notes that will help you to understand what to expect from your stay at a Wolsey Lodge.

Each Wolsey Lodge has its own page in this book which aims to give you a flavour of what you can look forward to when you stay there. On each page you will find out about your hosts and what facilities they have and whether the Lodge is suitable for children, if dogs are welcome, or if evening meals will be available to you.

Quietly comfortable, lavishly luxurious & always elegant

Wolsey Lodges will typically have a minimum of two bedrooms available for their guests, each usually made up with duvets, but please ask if you would prefer sheets and blankets.

Many hosts will provide tea, coffee, fruit juices and other lovely touches such as fruit and homemade biscuits in your room. Don't expect to find a fridge, however. Hosts will usually provide fresh milk when you need it.

All rooms will have en suite or private bathrooms (if the bathroom is private you'll normally find bathrobes waiting for you) but some may have either a shower or bath, so if you have a preference, please discuss it when you book. Towels and essential toiletries are usually all supplied.

If you are travelling with friends or relatives and are happy to share a bathroom with them, then your hosts may be able to accommodate you. It is always worth asking your hosts if there are rooms available during your stay so everyone in your party can be accommodated. Alternatively your hosts may be able to help you arrange accommodation for large parties at several closely located Lodges - so just ask.

In line with 'no smoking' legislation in England, Scotland and Wales, all Wolsey Lodge accommodation is 'smoke free' with the majority of houses showing the symbol ![symbol] which indicates that it is a No Smoking House. However, a small number of Wolsey Lodges show the ![symbol] symbol which means that whilst all rooms used by guests are totally smoke free, smoking is possible in other, private parts of the house.

Sleeping, showering or soaking in the bathtub - relaxation is assured

iv

Left: Letham House, East Lothian (Wolsey Lodge)

Wining & dining

The comfortable and elegant surroundings to be found at Wolsey Lodges is equalled only by the quality of the breakfasts that will follow your good night's sleep. Always fresh and often locally sourced or organic ingredients are offered, whether you opt for a light start to the day with fruit and cereals or plump for a hearty breakfast to see you through your day's activities.

Menus will vary considerably so please feel free to discuss your breakfast requirements with your hosts when you book especially if you have special dietary needs.

Joining us for dinner?

A long held tradition for Wolsey Lodge hosts is to offer their guests dinner at some point during their stay. Whilst for many Wolsey Lodges this tradition holds strong, the changing needs of guests mean that some will offer just a light supper, whilst others do not offer evening meals, but instead have a veritable array of nearby restaurants, bistros and pubs to recommend to their guests.

Some Wolsey Lodges are licensed to sell alcoholic drinks (look for the ▮ symbol in their entry) so lingering late over a final glass of fine port or aged brandy is not unusual. Prices for wine are generally as you would expect them to be in a pub and if the Lodge is not licensed, please check with your hosts about bringing your own alcohol. This is indicated by the BYO symbol in their entry.

If the Lodge you are staying at offers dinner or supper then you can expect a culinary treat in the company of other guests and sometimes your hosts as well. The number of courses and the nature of the evening meal will vary from Lodge to Lodge and this is reflected in the price.

Each Lodge is unique in what it offers and so we strongly recommend that you discuss your dining requirements with your host when you book to avoid later misunderstandings and disappointment. If you have agreed to 'dine in', then discuss with your hosts the exact nights you will be expecting dinner and any special dietary requirements that any member of your party has.

Your hosts will be able to offer you advice on the best places to eat.

Top: Old Whyly, East Sussex (Wolsey Lodge)

v

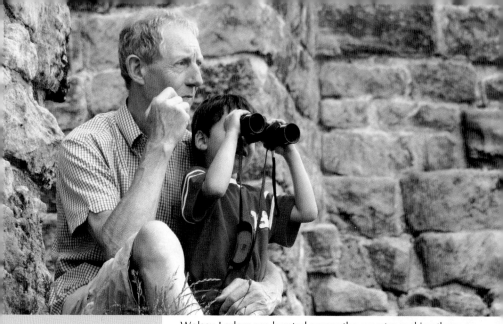

Visiting with your family - & the dog could come too.

Wolsey Lodges are located across the country making them an ideal base for touring an area. Some Wolsey Lodges welcome children although many will state a minimum age for their guests - this is shown on their entry page although it will always be at your hosts' discretion depending on the requirements of their other guests. It is essential you inform your hosts if there are children in your party.

If your hosts offer evening meals it is very possible that young children will not be able to dine with other guests, but your hosts may be able to provide a suitable meal at an earlier time for them or will suggest alternative venues. Wolsey Lodges that are suitable for children may offer cots and help with your baby (such as warming bottles and baby food in the kitchen) but it is essential that you discuss your requirements at the time of booking. Check too about price reductions for children, as these often apply!

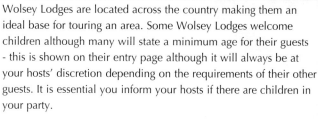

You will find three symbols in the Lodges' entries that denote their policy on dogs and/or pets at their house. The ⬛ symbol denotes that the house has no animals in it and do not take guests' dogs either. The ⬛ symbol denotes that the Lodge has their own pets in the house but do not take guests' dogs. Finally if you want to take your own dog(s) with you then please look for the ⬛ symbol. IMPORTANT NOTE - Even where this symbol appears, guests **must** discuss their requirements at the time of booking, as each Lodge will have their own policy about where in the house guests' pets can be taken - some Lodges do not allow dogs in the house and instead have kennels outside.

Left: Tuttington Hall, Norfolk (Wolsey Lodge)

Across to France

The magic of Wolsey Lodges can be found at an exclusive collection of Lodges in France.

These Lodges combine all the style, sophistication and hospitality that Wolsey Lodges has come to be known by, with easy continental charm; all located in some of the most idyllic and unspoilt areas of France.

Your hosts are all English-speaking and very knowledgeable about their areas to help you understand its history, culture, character and, of course, its cuisine.

Prices quoted on these members' pages will be in Euros and they will only accept payment in Sterling by prior arrangement. Please check the Sterling prices at the time of booking as exchange rates will vary.

Discover the magic of Wolsey Lodges across France

Reservations

Staying at a Wolsey Lodge is totally different to staying at an hotel and much of what makes a stay truly enjoyable comes from discussing your proposed visit with your hosts.

The easiest way to make your booking is by telephone which gives you the chance to check all of the details properly and ensure that you have chosen the right Lodge for your individual needs. Alternatively you can make a booking enquiry through the website (www.wolseylodges.com) by completing your details, required dates and your specific requirements. The individual Lodge will then contact you to progress your booking.

Booking is essential at all Wolsey Lodges as most will not accept guests without a pre-arranged booking.

Deposits

Your hosts will often ask for a non-refundable deposit to secure your booking, with the balance of payment due on departure.

Left: Long Crendon Manor, Buckinghamshire (Wolsey Lodge)

On arrival

Normal arrival time is between 4pm and 6pm. It is essential that you let your host know the time you plan to arrive particularly if your arrival is likely to be later than 6pm. It's also worth noting that your hosts may well be out during the day and will not expect to greet you before 4pm at the earliest unless you have made definite alternative arrangements with them. You are visiting your hosts' home so when you arrive please ring the bell if your host hasn't already seen you, rather than walking straight in.

Your planned arrival time is especially important if you have arranged to 'eat-in' on your first evening as meals are served at a set time and a late arrival may mean that you miss your meal completely. Delays on journeys are a trying annoyance but a call to your hosts to let them know of a delayed arrival is much appreciated and, whether you were planning to dine with them or not, it means they may be able to make alternative supper arrangements for you.

During your stay

If you are staying for a number of days, your hosts will still expect you to be out for most of the day as many of them will have work or shopping to do and will not have staff to attend to you in their absence. However, some are happy for you to spend your days around the Lodge to use the pool, tennis courts or perhaps to go walking, but please check this with your hosts carefully.

Departure

You will normally be expected to vacate your room by 11am at the latest on your day of departure.

White Horse at Uffington, Oxfordshire.

Cancellations

If you have to cancel your booking, please remember that a contract exists between you and the Wolsey Lodge that you have made your booking with. The Lodge will always try to re-let your cancelled accommodation, but your deposit will not normally be refunded due to the administration costs of making the initial booking and re-booking.

Wolsey Lodges recommend that all Lodges have a cancellation policy if they cannot re-let the accommodation you have booked. In these circumstances you will be liable for 30% of the total charge if you cancel within 28 days of the visit; 60% if you cancel within 13 days and 80% if you cancel within 48 hours.

Some Lodges may have their own cancellation policies that differ from this and this will be made clear to you when you make your reservation.

We do not operate a cancellation insurance scheme and strongly recommend that you take out your own appropriate cover.

Prices & our latest information

Prices

All prices shown on the Lodge information pages are per person, per night based on shared occupancy of a double or twin bedded room and include a generous 'Wolsey Lodge' breakfast. An extra charge is usually made for a double room used as a single, highlighted as 'Single supplement' or 'Single occupancy'. Reduced charges may apply for extended stays, so please check with the Lodge when booking. All prices are inclusive of VAT where applicable.

IMPORTANT - The prices shown in this brochure were correct at the time of going to print. We recommend that you confirm the prices when making your reservation. Where there is a price variance, Wolsey Lodges Ltd cannot be held responsible for any problem that may arise.

Visit our website

At www.wolseylodges.com you will find not only our complete brochure but a secure on-line shop where you can purchase gift vouchers as well as additional copies of this brochure. You will also find full details of any new Lodges joining our Collection there.

Easy to navigate maps will help you to select your Lodge and allow you to plan your journey whether you are visiting just one Lodge or several, in the UK or France. An automatic booking enquiry form enables you to complete your details and your preferred dates of travel, and your selected Lodge will then contact you to progress your booking.

New Lodges

This year we have 20 new Lodges for you to discover and enjoy. All their details can be found in the index section at the back of the brochure where they are highlighted.

Alternatively you can of course view their details by visiting www.wolseylodges.com and clicking on 'Discover New Lodges'.

Helping with a problem

All Lodges take their standards of quality very seriously and so, should a problem arise during your stay, or if you have any comments regarding quality at the Lodge you stay in, you must first inform your host so that they can attempt to put the problem right.

Choose your Wolsey Lodge

We have designed this brochure to be as simple as possible to use - whether you wish to search by region, by Lodge name and number, or by UK county or country.

The book is arranged by country and county so if you want to stay in a particular area, simply turn to that section of the book.

House Name	County	Entry No.
Trerose Manor	Cornwall	9

Finding your perfect Lodge is simple

Tessa & Piers Phipps
Trerose Manor, Mawnan Smith
Falmouth, Cornwall TR11 5HX
Tel: 01326 250784
info@trerosemanor.co.uk
www.trerosemanor.co.uk   2952

Finding Us
~ ' A20 from Exeter, then A39 ' ~

There is also a full index at the back of the brochure and Lodge entries are entered numerically starting with Lodge Entry Number 1. As well as identifying new members, for the first time the Index identifies Lodges that can help with wedding arrangements and also those where a group of guests may have exclusive use.

In recent years the collection has been enriched with Wolsey Lodges that were perhaps not simply homes. Those pages where the headings are in green, set out details of Wolsey Lodges where the owners have identified themselves as offering something a little different. These Lodges are also indentified in green in the Index. Whatever differences there are, all Wolsey Lodges remain very much under the personal supervision of their owners and offer the highest standards of hospitality.

The Lodge Entry Numbers will change for each edition of this brochure but one number will always stay the same - this is the four digit booking reference number on each Lodge's page which can be found just below the address and contact numbers.
You can use this number when making a booking in the future but we do recommend you get a new edition of this brochure when it has expired to ensure you are referring to the most up to date information available.

On our website www.wolseylodges.com you will find a series of easy-to-use, detailed maps to show exactly where each Lodge is located.

Top: Wollaston Lodge, Shropshire (Wolsey Lodge)

Special offers

and so much more

There is something quite wonderfully decadent about taking a weekend break at short notice. Stepping out of your everyday world, re-charging your batteries and seeing and experiencing something a little out of the ordinary. Take a short, or long, break to any Wolsey Lodge and you will not only discover beautiful houses but also kind, attentive hosts who warmly welcome you into their homes.

Our e-Newsletter will continue to keep you informed throughout the year. You've particulary appreciated the highlights we have given to Lodges that may be offering something a little different such as special menus as local, seasonal produce becomes available, open garden days, Christmas and New Year invitations and late-availability breaks. We've also given readers new ideas for unusual places to visit and updates about new Wolsey Lodges to try.

To register for our e-Newsletter simply email info@wolseylodges.com

From top: Three Cliffs Bay, Gower Peninsula; Prawles Court, East Sussex (Wolsey Lodge); Stoberry House, Somerset (Wolsey Lodge)

Could your home be a Wolsey Lodge?

Wolsey Lodges was started by a group of like-minded owners in 1981. Since then we have built a reputation for the quality of our houses and, most importantly, the level of hospitality we offer our guests.

Individuality, quality, consistency, quiet elegance, comfort, attention to detail, a warm, friendly welcome - these are all the things we value and which we know make the ultimate difference to a guest's experience. Our Lodge owners come from all walks of life - individuals, couples, families - all with varying outlooks, hobbies and lifestyles. Some of our hosts have jobs away from the home, some work from home and others are retired, but they still all share a real dedication to ensuring their guests have a memorable time.

This dedication to our guests, the exceptional accommodation we offer combined with outstanding cuisine, have all contributed to building our excellent reputation.

If you already run a B&B or think that your home and your hospitality might be what our guests are looking for, we would be delighted to send you a copy of our prospectus.

Ideally you will need to have a minimum of two guest bedrooms (4 bed spaces), each with their own bathroom, preferably en suite. Whilst some Wolsey Lodges still offer the option of dinner or supper every night, many offer it only occasionally, while others opt not to offer evening meals at all, which means you have total flexibility about what you offer.

Please visit our website www.wolseylodges.com for full details or contact our administration office on 01473 822058 for a prospectus and application form. We look forward to hearing from you.

Top: Domaine de la Freynelle, France (Wolsey Lodge)

WELCOME TO ENGLAND

Fabulous historic cities and towns, great country houses and gardens, bustling seaside resorts, picturesque villages, and miles and miles of beautiful countryside and coastline await your discovery throughout England.

Shopping, relaxing, exploring history, the best cuisine in the wo - England has it all. Whichever area of England you choose to visit there will be far more to take in than time will ever allow. Rest assured though that your hosts' intimate knowledge of their area means that you will get first-hand, on-the-spot advice of the very best that there is to experience.

From top: King's College Chapel, Cambridgeshire; Birling Gap, East Sussex; Roman Baths, Bath

Sue Soar
Long Crendon Manor
Frogmore Lane, Long Crendon
Aylesbury, Buckinghamshire
HP18 9DZ
Tel: 01844 201647 or 07867 521399
sue.soar@longcrendonmanor.co.uk
www.longcrendonmanor.co.uk 4986

The Property

Visitors to Long Crendon Manor will find themselves stepping back in time to undoubtedly one of the oldest Wolsey Lodges to be found. Dating back to 1187 when it began life as the dwelling for the abbots of Notley, the east and west wings were added in later centuries before a total refurbishment began in 1920.

Sue Soar and friendly St Bernard Coco will welcome you with tea and homemade biscuits. The delightful guest rooms are spacious and cosy and each has an en suite bathroom. As well as tea, coffee and a carafe of sherry, a fridge is filled with treats (some complimentary and some charged). Supremely comfortable beds are adorned with fine linen and goose down duvets. One bedroom has an adjoining dressing room which could be used as a twin for children – ideal for a family. Ask about the price for this.

Outside the gardens include a maze, croquet lawn and swimming pool; a vegetable and fruit garden, meadow and Sue's collection of rare breed pigs. Guests can use the oak-panelled drawing room to relax, read, watch television or just enjoy the log fire on a cold winter's night. Breakfast is served in the beamed dining room off the medieval hall and in the summer can be served on the terrace beneath the vine.

The Hosts

Sue had a successful career as a hotelier and now dedicates herself to Long Crendon Manor and breeds traditional English rare-breed pigs. Tim runs his own interim executive business, and they have three children.

The Location

Long Crendon Manor is unique and has been used in many TV productions including Midsomer Murders. Close by is Waddesdon Manor, Oxford Botanic Gardens, Bicester Village, Claydon House, Blenheim Palace, Stowe Gardens, Oxfordshire Golf Club, the Ashmolean Museum, Bletchley Park and the University of Oxford.

Finding Us

From M40 Junction 8a, follow A418 towards Aylesbury. On outskirts of Thame at services roundabout take B4011 to Long Crendon. First left in the village at The Square and continue down Frogmore Lane. Long Crendon Manor stone archway is 50 yards on left.

Rooms (per person per night incl. breakfast)

1 Super King (6') Four Poster Room (en suite)	£67.50
1 King Size (5') Room (en suite)	£60
1 Family Double (4'6") with Twin (2 x 3') Room (en suite)	£60
Single Occupancy	£80-£100

Meals

Dinner	£30

Opening Times

Occasionally closed Christmas

Payment Options

Facilities & Services

His Honour Judge & Mrs Richard Foster
Westend House
Cheddington, Leighton Buzzard
Buckinghamshire LU7 0RP
Tel: 01296 661332
westend.house@hotmail.com   **4983**
www.westendhousecheddington.co.uk

Finding Us

From North exit M1 J13. From Leighton Buzzard take B488 to Ivinghoe/Tring. After Horton turn right, over railway bridge and over mini roundabouts. After 300yds turn left. Westend House is on right. From South exit M1 J8 or M25 J20 along A41. From Tring take A4251 to Berkhamsted. Turn left into Cow Lane, follow signs to Tring station. After station turn left to Ivinghoe. Straight over roundabout and at T junction turn right. At Pitstone roundabout turn left, under railway bridge, turn right. Go over canal bridge, through Cheddington village to mini roundabouts, turn left. After 300 yds turn left. Westend House is on right.

The Property

Westend House is red brick and timber-framed, originally three Tudor cottages, now a fabulous family home. It is situated 10 miles east of Aylesbury, bordering Hertfordshire and Bedfordshire, in the ancient village of Cheddington in Buckinghamshire.

Guests can't fail to be impressed by its wonderful garden, with rose swags, vibrant herbaceous borders, wildlife pond and unique sculptures. Tea and homemade cake is served to visitors on arrival, by the inglenook in the cheerful drawing room or in the garden, depending on the season. The house is beautifully furnished and adorned with many watercolours and fascinating ancient maps.

Breakfast (and supper by prior arrangement) is served in the conservatory dining room overlooking the garden. Bedrooms – one in the main house with magnificent views of fields where the owner's sheep graze, the other in the adjoining barn conversion with private sitting room - have en suite bathrooms, televisions, hospitality trays and goose down pillows and duvets.

Rooms (per person per night incl. breakfast)

1 King Size (5') Room	(en suite)	**£45**
1 Double (4'6") Room	(en suite)	**£45**
Single Supplement		**£25**

Meals

Supper (2 courses)	**£17.50**

Opening Times

Closed Christmas & Easter

Payment Options

Facilities & Services

The Hosts

Richard, a Circuit Judge, combines this with caring for their rare breed livestock and gardening alongside Sue, a retired teacher. He is a keen golfer and enjoys opera and collecting wine. Guests will appreciate Sue's passion and skill in cooking, using home produced meat, vegetables and homemade preserves. Local hostelries are recommended for guests wishing to dine out.

The Location

Cheddington, dating back to the Domesday Book, is in the Chiltern Hills and has its own station, with fast trains to London in only 45 minutes, making this an ideal location for city dwellers fancying a Wolsey Lodge country break. Its proximity to major trunk roads and the M1 makes it a great stopover for travellers too, but it is also the perfect base to explore an abundance of National Trust properties and walks.

Anthony & Alison O'Connor
Tregoose,
Grampound, Truro, Cornwall TR2 4DB
Tel: 01726 882460
Fax: 01872 222427
tregoose@tregoose.co.uk
www.tregoose.co.uk   **2995**

Finding Us

Leave A30 by turning left for Grampound Road. Continue 5 miles through Grampound Road. Turn right at junction with A390 towards Truro. The lane leading to drive is after 200 yards, on right, just where double white lines end in centre of road; lane entrance is between four black and white reflector posts.

The Property

This elegant and comfortable 1830s Cornish country house stands in the rolling countryside of the Roseland peninsula.

Alison and friendly Border Terrier, Tamar, greet guests and after showing them to their rooms, serves tea in the guest's drawing room.

The three guest bedrooms, all with their own generous bathrooms, are comfortable, inviting and prettily decorated, with superb views over the beautiful two acre garden.

This is Alison's first love and she delights in showing guests around. She has restored and enlarged it meticulously over the last twenty years. It contains many rare and interesting plants, a sunken, herbaceous walled garden, a croquet lawn and a recently laid-out potager.

The Hosts

Anthony has spent much of his professional life in East Africa and the Far East and has recently retired from his own law firm in Truro. He is a keen sailor and golfer.

Alison has practised horticulture and garden design all her professional life. She holds a NDH and is an authority on Cornish plants and gardens. She will also happily recommend interesting places and restaurants to visit.

The Location

Tregoose is centrally situated for the whole county - from the Tate at St Ives and Land's End to houses and gardens on the Devon border - all are within an hour's drive. The great gardens of Caerhays, Heligan, Trewithen and the Eden Project are all within five miles and beaches, sailing waters and the coastal footpath are easily reached.

Rooms (per person per night incl. breakfast)

2 King Size (5') Rooms (1 en suite/1 private)	£49-£63
1 Twin (2 x 3') Room (en suite)	£55-£63
Single Supplement	£20

Meals

Dinner	£32

Opening Times

Closed Christmas, New Year & Easter

Payment Options

Facilities & Services

The Property

Not content with being a gloriously restored Victorian house offering every modern comfort and luxury, Penarwyn is also the home of the most welcoming and delightful hosts one could wish to meet. Jan and Mike have created a wonderfully peaceful haven that is beautifully furnished and finished with careful attention to detail, which is reflected in the unsurpassed standard of service they offer their guests. Their aim is to make your stay so enjoyable and unforgettable that you will want to return again and again – and they certainly succeed in that.

From the first glimpse of the house from the driveway, the view of the gardens displaying a wide variety of native and sub tropical trees and shrubs, it is clear this is something special. The bedrooms and bathrooms are superbly furnished, offering televisions, DVD/CD players, tea and coffee making facilities, hairdryers, and luxurious baths and showers with fine linen, towels and robes. The drawing room has comfortable furniture, a Boudoir Grand piano and French doors opening onto the glazed veranda and guests are welcome to use the billiards room with its selection of books, games and puzzles. Breakfast at Penarwyn is award winning, freshly cooked and definitely not to be missed.

The Hosts

Mike and Jan entered the hotel industry in the early 1990's and have brought those years of experience to Penarwyn. Their skills in interior design and carpentry are evident throughout the house. They 'go the extra mile', from arranging pick ups for guests arriving by train and helping to plan days out to recommending local restaurants for dinner – nothing is too much trouble.

The Location

Perfect for the Eden Project, The Lost Gardens of Heligan, Lanhydrock House, and Carlyon Bay golf course. Visit Lostwithiel, Fowey, Charlestown, St Mawes and the Roseland Peninsula, Padstow and Lands End.

Mike & Jan Russell
Penarwyn House
St Blazey
Par
Cornwall PL24 2DS
Tel: 01726 814224
info@penarwyn.co.uk
www.penarwyn.co.uk   2968

Finding Us

From the A390 at St Blazey turn into Doubletrees school, drive down past the school, Penarwyn is directly in front of you.

Rooms (per person per night incl. breakfast)

3 Super King (6')/Twin Rooms (en suite)	**£55-£80**
Single Supplement for Super King or Twin Rooms	**£30**

Meals

Breakfast only

Opening Times

Closed Christmas & New Year

Payment Options

Facilities & Services

The Property

'Luxury B&B meets family run boutique hotel' best describes Pentillie Castle. The splendour and comfort of this property is second to none. Arrive through parkland, an abundance of walks and views across Dartmoor to discover the perfectly sumptuous bedrooms, gardens and dining that await, and you may wish to lose yourself here and never leave.

The castle started life as a grand formal house in 1698 and was gradually enlarged and used for different purposes throughout the following centuries before it was inherited and restored by hosts Ted and Sarah Coryton. Almost 55 acres of park, woodland and garden surround the castle including a heated outdoor pool and an American garden abundant with rhododendrons, camellias, magnolias and azaleas. Inside, large though it is, there is a welcoming, homely feel overlaid with an unmistakable historic grandeur.

Each guest room is luxurious, comfortable and spacious. Home cooked suppers are available to order in advance from an extensive menu, which can be enjoyed in the 'farmhouse' kitchen, dining room or on the terraces. Pentillie Castle is unlike any other Wolsey Lodge and a real treasure to visit.

The Hosts

Ted and Sarah's love of Pentillie is clear in the work they have done to make it their home and guests are made to feel so welcome to share it with them and nothing is too much trouble – just ask. Ted is a former helicopter pilot and still works as an aviation and oil exploration consultant and Sarah is a clinical massage therapist.

The Location

Exploring and enjoying the grounds here will take time, make sure you visit the newly restored Mausoleum and walled kitchen garden. Close by are river trips on the Tamar, Bodmin Moor and Dartmoor, The Eden Project, National Trust properties and of course, the splendour of Cornish gardens aplenty.

Mr & Mrs Ted Coryton
Pentillie Castle
St Mellion, Saltash
Cornwall PL12 6QD
Tel: 01579 350044
contact@pentillie.co.uk
www.pentillie.co.uk   2962

Finding Us

Take A38 into Cornwall. At first roundabout, turn right onto A388, signed to Callington and Launceston. Follow road for 3.1 miles, to Paynters Cross. Turn right signed Paynters Cross, Cargreen and Landulph. Pentillie Castle gates are within 100 yards of main road.

Rooms (per person per night incl. breakfast)

4 Super King (6')/Twin Rooms (en suite)	**£60-£120**
1 Four Poster Super King (6') (en suite)	**£90-£100**
Single Occupancy – £15 less than best available room rate	

Meals

Supper (By prior arrangement)	from **£18**

Opening Times

Open all year

Payment Options

Facilities & Services

The Property

Set amidst 3½ acres overlooking the oak woodland of Carminowe Valley, this tranquil eighteenth century farmhouse is within earshot of the sea and is centrally placed between both peninsulas of South West Cornwall.

In the beamed sitting room a stylish log burner in the large inglenook blazes on cooler days when guests can sink into deep comfortable sofas adorned by colourful cushions. Antiques, books and flowers mingle with watercolours and finely chosen contemporary art which reflect Marion's interests - she can advise on local galleries, auctions and gardens. The effortless chic continues upstairs in a restful bedroom which overlooks the walled front garden. The private bathroom has a free standing bath and separate shower, thick towels and organic toiletries.

Rambling roses cascade down steps into the valley with its babbling brook. On through the woodland walk, around the large pond, crossing bridges, through the orchard and kitchen garden to the summer house - Mazey Cottage is a gardener's delight. Guests are welcome to enjoy the garden at any time, seats are dotted throughout from where endless wildlife can be observed.

The Hosts

Peter and Marion are relaxed outgoing hosts, their friendly manner puts guests at ease. Peter, a retired businessman is keen on cycling, walking and kayaking, Marion's passion is her garden and she can advise on garden visits. Together their local knowledge will make your stay memorably enjoyable.

The Location

Surrounded by the National Trust woodlands, the sea, Loe Bar and Loe Pool (Cornwall's largest lake) are a ten minute walk. Nearby are Godolphin House, Trebah and Glendurgan Gardens, St Michaels Mount, Minack Theatre, Tate St Ives and Falmouth Maritime Museum. Water sports can be arranged for day sailing, canoeing, fishing or surfing.

Mr & Mrs Peter Stanley
Mazey Cottage
Tangies
Gunwalloe
Helston
Cornwall TR12 7PU
Tel: 01326 565868
stanley.m2@sky.com
www.mazeycottage.co.uk   2960

Finding Us

A3083 Helston-Lizard. After 1 mile turn right immediately behind central bollards. Do not go under the bridge. Narrow steep lane for ¾ mile, house on the right at the bottom of the valley.

Rooms (per person per night incl. breakfast)

1 King Size (5') Room (private)	**£45-£55**
Single Supplement	**£15**

Meals

Supper	**£25**

Opening Times

Closed Christmas & New Year

Payment Options

Facilities & Services

The Property

Creed House is everything this beautiful part of the country offers. Set in seven acres of gardens, this spacious Georgian house was once home to the local rector before it became the family home of your hosts Annabel and Jonathon Croggon. Interestingly Titanium was discovered here.

Antiques, pictures and plates adorn the rooms and the use of beautiful fabrics around the home is testament to Annabel's background as an interior designer. A private staircase leads to the two guests rooms, between which is a guest sitting room replete with reading material and guides of the local area and sitting here awhile in front of the warming fire is an utter delight. Each guest bedroom has an en suite bathroom amply supplied with potions and lotions with which to indulge.

The gardens are tranquil with a walled garden and many specimen trees, shrubs and ponds. A choice of continental or traditional breakfast is offered and a fine array of local restaurants and pubs cater for all tastes for dinner. All in all, Creed House is the perfect Wolsey Lodge and you will be made to feel most welcome in a beautiful home.

The Hosts

Annabel and Jonathon took over the house from his parents who moved into a house in the grounds. Annabel now devotes her time to looking after her children, home, garden and guests whilst Jonathon works nearby as a stockbroker. They both enjoy travel and history when time allows.

The Location

In the heart of Cornwall, Creed House is 'local' to so much – the coast is under five miles away, Heligan, Eden, Trewithen, Caerhays, St Mawes, Trelissick, Truro, Padstow, St Ives, Penzance, Helford River, Minnack Theatre, Trerice House, Lanhydrock House and Pencarrow House to name just a few places to visit.

Annabel & Jonathon Croggon
Creed House
Creed
Grampound
Truro
Cornwall
TR2 4SL
Tel: 01872 530372
jrcroggon@btinternet.com
www.creedhouse.co.uk   2958

Finding Us

From Truro take A390 towards St Austell, after 7 miles you will reach Grampound. Half way up hill, just before the clock tower take right turn to Creed. After approx. 1 mile and just after the church left at the oak tree. The entrance to Creed House is second white gate on left.

Rooms (per person per night incl. breakfast)

1 Super King (6') Room (en suite)	**£50-£55**
1 Super King (6')/Twin (en suite)	**£50-£55**
Single Supplement	**£50-£55**

Meals

Breakfast only

Opening Times

Closed Christmas & New Year

Payment Options

Facilities & Services

The Property

As sensational locations go, Bay House may take some beating. Situated above Housel Bay on Cornwall's Lizard Peninsula, this stunning Wolsey Lodge occupies the most southerly location in England with miles of mesmerising ocean beyond. Just a short walk from the Lizard lighthouse, the garden drops down to the cliff footpath and direct access to the beach and many miles of coastal walking.

Bay House was built in the 1920s and the light, bright rooms take advantage of the dramatic coastline views and sea beyond. Antique and contemporary furniture complement the neutral shades of the décor whilst the soft furnishings reflect the bright, crisp colours of the house's surroundings. There are three extremely comfortable guest rooms, each with sea views. Ideal for relaxing and taking in the ever changing vista.

In the garden there are flowers normally native to far warmer climes but which happily thrive here due to its southerly, warmer location and the summer house and other seating areas are perfect on warmer days as somewhere to enjoy afternoon tea.

Breakfast is served in the open-plan dining area which has great views. Dinner too can be enjoyed, by arrangement, and of course fish is the local speciality. There are also local restaurants aplenty.

The Hosts

Carla and John moved to Bay House in 2010. Carla is Dutch and met John when he was working in Holland. John is now retired and is the resident 'cook'. They enjoy tennis, golf, art and painting.

The Location

As well as many National Trust gardens and houses in the vicinity, guests can also enjoy the Goonhilly Satellite Earth Station, the Museum of Submarine Telegraphy, Land's End, windsurfing in Coverack, The Lizard Peninsula, Sennen Cove, St. Michael's Mount, Lizard Lighthouse Heritage Centre, St Ives and Lizard Wireless Station.

John & Carla Caslin
Bay House
Housel Bay
The Lizard
Cornwall
TR12 7PG
Tel: 01326 290235 or 07740 168805
carla.caslin@btinternet.com
www.mostsoutherlypoint.co.uk   2956

Finding Us

From Helston take A3083 to The Lizard. In centre of Lizard village turn left - past row of houses on left and football pitch on right. After 500 yards take first turning right. Follow this road to very end, turn right onto short unmade road signed to Bay House. Turn left at green garage.

Rooms (per person per night incl. breakfast)

1 Twin (2 x 3') Atlantic Room (en suite)	**£82.50**
1 Twin (2 x 3') Quarterdeck Room (en suite)	**£72.50**
1 Super King (6') Ocean Breeze Room (private)	**£72.50**

Meals

Supper	**£35**

Opening Times

Closed Christmas

Payment Options

Facilities & Services

Tessa & Piers Phipps
Trerose Manor, Mawnan Smith
Falmouth, Cornwall TR11 5HX
Tel: 01326 250784
info@trerosemanor.co.uk
www.trerosemanor.co.uk   **2952**

Finding Us
Take A30 from Exeter, then A39 to Truro towards Falmouth. At Treliever roundabout (large double roundabout) take 2nd turning (unmarked) off 2nd roundabout through Mabe Burnthouse. In Mawnan Smith, bear left at Red Lion Pub, go ½ mile up hill, turn right into Old Church Road (sign behind you). After ½ mile you will see Trerose Farm (a working farm) on the right. Trerose Manor is immediately beyond the Farm on right, look out for large white gate & Post Box in wall. Newquay Airport ~ 45 minutes; Truro Rail Station ~ 30 minutes; Falmouth Branch Rail Station ~ 10 minutes

The Property
Trerose Manor is situated close to the mouth of the Helford River and offers the perfect base from which to explore this beautiful part of Cornwall.

Strategically positioned, this ancient site is thought to date from the Bronze Age and parts of the house date back to the 13th century. On arrival visitors enjoy marvellous views across Falmouth Bay and then drive down a veritable tunnel of mimosa and yew, emerging in front of the house.

The historic house provides sumptuous accommodation with a fascinating range of antiques and pictures. Fresh flowers, books and magazines abound. Each bedroom is generously proportioned, with comfortable seating and en suite bathroom, flat screen television, hairdryer, tea and coffee making facilities plus a range of toiletries.

A traditional Cornish cream tea is offered on arrival, which, like the delicious breakfast, is served in the cosy kitchen or on the terrace. Produce is locally sourced wherever possible. Celebratory dinners can be arranged when booking all three rooms, please discuss at time of booking.

The Hosts
The home of the Phipps family, Tessa and Piers have lived at Trerose for 35 years and while relatively new to hosting, they have rapidly built up a loyal clientele of return visitors.

Having spent most of their working life based in London before settling back in Cornwall full time, they thoroughly enjoy welcoming guests and delight in sharing their detailed knowledge and love of the area, and suggesting local walks. They are justifiably proud of their fabulous, quintessentially Cornish garden which guests are free to enjoy and paint!

The Location
This part of Cornwall has so much to offer. Whatever your interests, visiting beautiful gardens or historical National Trust properties, art galleries or simply enjoying the wonderful coastal scenery, everything is within easy reach. Trerose is also a walkers' paradise with a superlative choice right on the doorstep. St Ives, St Michael's Mount and the Lizard Peninsular are just a short drive away.

Rooms (per person per night incl. breakfast)

3 King Size (5') Rooms (en suite)	**£65-£70**
Single Supplement	**£20**

Meals
Breakfast only

Opening Times
Closed occasionally

Payment Options

Facilities & Services

Steven & Jane Epperson
Anchorage House
Nettles Corner, Tregrehan
St Austell, Cornwall PL25 3RH
Tel: 01726 814071
info@anchoragehouse.co.uk
www.anchoragehouse.co.uk　　2994

Finding Us

From Exeter take A30 through Devon & Cornwall. About 10 miles after Bodmin exit, turn left onto A391 St. Austell exit for about 8 miles to St Austell to A390. Turn left (away from St. Austell onto A390). After 500 yards look for the brown 'Anchorage House' tourist sign and turn left across from the St. Austell Garden Centre towards Tregrehan village & then immediately left again into driveway that leads past three other houses and through gate to Anchorage House's courtyard.

Rooms　(per person per night incl. breakfast)

3 Super King (6') Rooms (en suite)	**£55-£67.50**

Meals

Supper　(1 course)	**£20**
Dinner　(2 courses)	**£25**

Opening Times

Closed December to February

Payment Options

The Property

Anchorage House is an impressive Georgian style Wolsey Lodge offering guests the perfect luxury escape in the heart of Cornwall. This exceptional Wolsey Lodge is home to Steve and Jane Epperson who offer their guests a very special experience including use of the heated indoor lap swimming pool, hot tub and small gym.

There are two guest lounges and candlelight suppers can also be enjoyed by prior arrangement. Every attention to detail is evident throughout this beautiful house and in particular the three individually designed guest bedrooms which are stunning. As you would expect the en suite bathrooms are ultra modern with everything you could wish for including invigorating power showers and huge free-standing baths. The easy mix of elegant and modern styling throughout the house is delightful and it works.

The house has manicured gardens both to the front and rear and there is an outside 'chill out' lounge off the courtyard for relaxation after a day out exploring the area.

The Hosts

With their previous experience of running a country house hotel, Jane and Steve, a retired Special Operations Commander and Commanding Officer in the U.S. Navy, have struck the perfect balance between high end luxury and personal home comforts. They are genuinely committed to ensuring that Wolsey Lodge guests have a special and unforgettable stay, starting with afternoon tea and homemade cake on arrival.

The Location

Anchorage House is just five minutes from the Eden Project and Carlyon Bay beach and golf, and fifteen minutes from the Lost Gardens of Heligan, Fowey and Mevagissey fishing harbours. Jane and Steve are very knowledgeable of the surrounding area and all that Cornwall has to offer so will make sure that their Wolsey Lodge guests don't miss any places of interest.

Facilities & Services

Geoff & Jessica French
Molesworth Manor
Little Petherick
Padstow
Cornwall PL27 7QT
Tel: 01841 540292
molesworthmanor@aol.com
www.molesworthmanor.co.uk   2945

Finding Us

Located off the A389 between Wadebridge and Padstow. Entrance is clearly signed, 300 yards from the bridge in Little Petherick. The nearest train station is Bodmin Parkway which is on the Paddington to Penzance Line.

The Property

A fabulous, child-friendly Wolsey Lodge, just a stone's throw from Padstow, is the perfect base for exploring North Cornwall. Originally a Grade II listed rectory, with parts dating from the 17th century, it is now a lovely family home, offering a warm welcome and furnished in a mix of antique and contemporary with interesting works of art.

In lovely grounds packed with unusual, indigenous Cornish plants and shrubs, this granite and slate home has eight guest rooms situated on the first and second floors offering a mix of bed size. Bedrooms are individually furnished to a very high standard with televisions, folders packed with local information and a hospitality tray. There are two guest lounges, with open fires on cooler days, and an honesty bar.

Delicious breakfasts are served at separate tables, with a full English as well as different daily specials. The majority of produce is locally sourced or homemade, and the white chocolate muffins, selection of breads and Geoff's marmalade are legendary!

Rooms (per person per night incl. breakfast)

1 Super King (6')/Twin Room (en suite)	**£64**
2 King Size (5') Rooms (en suite)	**£64**
5 Double (4'6") Rooms (en suite)	**£59-£64**
Single Occupancy	**£96**

Meals

Breakfast only

Opening Times

Closed 31st October - 1st February

Payment Options

Facilities & Services

The Hosts

Geoff's background is computer sales and Jessica, formerly in conference and incentive travel, enjoys gardening, ceramic design and art - evident throughout their home. Geoff is a keen golfer and can organise golf for guests. With their two young sons they enjoy sharing local knowledge and are pleased to advise on the excellent local restaurants and pubs.

The Location

Nearby Padstow is 'foodie heaven' and local seafood is a speciality. With glorious beaches for water sports, breathtaking scenery, coastal routes for walking and cycling, and excellent golf courses, this is the perfect location n this beautiful part of Cornwall. The Eden Project, a wealth of gardens and National Trust properties are within easy reach.

Helen McCall & Philip Ranshaw
Hideaway at Herrington Hill, High Lane,
Newbottle, County Durham DH4 4NH
Tel: 07730 957795 or 07767 353236
info@hideawayatherringtonhill.co.uk **8938**
www.hideawayatherringtonhill.com

Finding Us

From A1 J62 turn onto A690 towards
Sunderland. Continue for 5 miles then turn
left onto High Lane towards Newbottle for
0.2 miles, then right onto Herrington Hill
which is signed Private Road. Hideaway
is on the left immediately past St. George
Flag. Electric gates ahead with an entry/
intercom system on left pillar. From A19
head towards Durham on A690. Carry on
0.6 Miles then right onto High Lane towards
Newbottle for 0.2 Miles, then right onto
Herrington Hill which is signed Private
Road. Hideaway on left immediately past
St. George flag. Electric Gates ahead with an
entry/intercom system on left pillar.

The Property

Hideaway at Herrington Hill is a Georgian hunting lodge
in the village of Newbottle, County Durham and was built
in 1838 for the Earl of Durham. It is set in three acres of
mature gardens and is approached through rolling farmland
before arriving at a gravelled courtyard.

Sympathetically refurbished, many of the original features
remain and the style is classical with some contemporary
touches. The spacious guest bedrooms have en suite or
private bathrooms (one with slipper bath and garden views).
After a busy day exploring the area, guests can choose to
relax in the lounge or the morning room, both exclusively
for guests use, or perhaps on one of several patio areas.

Delicious breakfasts are served in the hunting-themed country
dining room, with refectory style table, striking crimson walls,
antique furniture and interesting paintings. There is a wide
range of options for breakfast including the usual full English
or smoked salmon and scrambled eggs. All ingredients are
top quality and locally sourced wherever possible.

The Hosts

Hideaway has been Philip and Helen's home for many
years and after their children left home, they decided
to refurbish the property and become a luxury bed and
breakfast. Retired dental surgeon Philip enjoys shooting,
sailing and fine wines, while Helen loves cooking,
entertaining and making new friends. The welcome is
second to none and both go out of their way to look after
their guests. There are several excellent pubs just a short
drive away (or a longer walk).

The Location

Being within 10 minutes from the A1 this is perfectly placed
for easy access to Durham, Sunderland, Newcastle and the
North East Coast. Other attractions include the Beamish
Museum and Hadrian's Wall. Three golf clubs, fishing lakes
and several famous pheasant shoots are also nearby.

Rooms (per person per night incl. breakfast)

1 King Size (5') Room	(private)	**£60**
2 Double (4'6") Rooms	(en suite)	**£50**
Single Supplement		**£50-£60**

Meals

Breakfast only

Opening Times

Open all year

Payment Options

Facilities & Services

The Property

Dowfold House, a charming Victorian house in the heart of County Durham, once the local mine manager's residence, now offers the very warmest of welcomes. This 'home from home', is near to the North Pennines Area of Outstanding Natural Beauty and has attractive grounds with views over the Wear Valley. Ample parking is available and overnight stabling next door for guests travelling with their horse.

Drive through stone gateposts, park by wisteria clad outhouses and be welcomed by your hosts. Then enjoy tea and home-made biscuits in the cosy guest sitting room, conservatory or patio, depending on the weather. Classically furnished, every nook and cranny houses part of an eclectic book collection. Enjoy an award winning breakfast in the elegant dining room, which is adorned with portraits of family forebears.

The bedrooms are individually furnished and all with en suite facilities and pleasant views. Quality linen, great showers, tea/coffee tray with home-made goodies, stylish toiletries and flat screen digital televisions all make for a restful stay.

The Hosts

Jill and Rupert bought Dowfold House eight years ago as a going concern. Much tender loving care has since been lavished - and it shows. Guests appreciate Rupert's background in baking and catering and Jill's natural affinity with hospitality and attention to detail. Jill is the gardener, while Rupert enjoys singing with the local choral society. Environmental issues are close to their hearts and the household is run with a green ethos.

The Location

Just nine miles from Durham and being half way between London and Inverness, it is a great stopping off place. Those staying a while will find the area steeped in history, heritage and the most inspiring scenery. Hadrian's Wall, Newcastle's Blinking Eye bridge, the oldest Saxon church in the UK, Gateshead's Angel of the North and the wild windswept North Pennines are all easily accessible.

Jill & Rupert Richardson
Dowfold House
Low Jobs Hill
Crook
County Durham DL15 9AB
Tel: 01388 762473
enquiries@dowfoldhouse.co.uk
www.dowfoldhouse.co.uk   8937

Finding Us

Directions available at time of booking.

Rooms (per person per night incl. breakfast)

1 King Size (5') Room (en suite)	from **£40**
1 Double (4'6") Room (en suite)	from **£38**
1 Twin (2 x 3') Room (en suite)	from **£38**
Single Occupancy	from **£55**

Meals

Breakfast only

Opening Times

Closed Christmas & New Year

Payment Options

Facilities & Services

David and Angela Carr
Sirelands,
Heads Nook, Brampton,
Cumbria CA8 9BT
Tel: 01228 670389
carr_sirelands@btconnect.com   **8975**

Finding Us

From M6 Junction 43 take A69 for
Newcastle. After 3 miles turn right at traffic
lights for Heads Nook (1½ miles). After
village pass two junctions. Keep right at letter
box, signposted Castle Carrock. 1 mile on,
white house on left.

The Property

In this quiet, unsung corner of Cumbria, you will find
Sirelands, a beautiful, sheltered and peaceful Cumbrian
cottage overlooking the North Pennines, yet only ten
minutes from the nearest M6 junction at Carlisle.

Guests are welcomed into this relaxing home with home
baked afternoon tea, served in front of the open fire or in
the summerhouse, depending on the season. Settle into
a comfortable sofa in the large, traditionally decorated
drawing room overlooking the garden. Throughout the
house is a wealth of browsing material and bedtime reading
for bookworms to enjoy.

Charming guest rooms, overlooking the garden, include
a twin with extra long beds and a double with traditional
style sleigh bed, offering tea and coffee making facilities and
television. Both bathrooms, one en suite, the other a few
steps from the double room have baths with showers over.

A secluded garden with tranquil pond and stream is home
to roe deer and a wide variety of birds including families
of wild ducks, while beyond are woodland walks with
impressive displays of bluebells and foxgloves to gladden
the heart in spring and summer.

The Hosts

David and Angela have farmed here since 1962 and have
derived enormous pleasure from developing Sirelands,
which has evolved from a traditional gardener's cottage
dating from about 1730. They enjoy country pursuits
available in the area and entertaining guests has always
been an essential and enjoyable part of their lives.

The Location

The Lake District and Hadrians Wall are particular
attractions, but there is also golf, fishing, the RSPB Reserve at
Geltsdale and regular meetings at Carlisle race course. The
city of Carlisle has many historic interests of its own.

Rooms (per person per night incl. breakfast)

1 King Size (5') Room	(private)	**£50**
1 Twin (2 x 3') Room	(en suite)	**£50**
Single Supplement		**£10**

Meals

Supper	**£22**
Dinner	**£27.50**

Opening Times

Closed Christmas & New Year

Payment Options

Facilities & Services

Gerry & Marion Bobbett
St Mary's Mount
Belmont, Ulverston
Cumbria LA12 7HD
Tel: 01229 583372 or 07734 849005
gerry.bobbett@virgin.net
www.stmarysmount.co.uk   8970

The Property

Original Victorian features greet guests on arrival as well as a warm welcome from hosts Gerry and Marion. Dating back to 1825, the manor house sits in ¾ of an acre of peaceful walled gardens with wide-reaching views across Ulverston and Morecambe Bay. Rich in Victorian style, including original fireplaces in each bedroom, and furnished with graceful antiques, guests have a private lounge and conservatory that benefit from the glorious sea views. Bedrooms are large and combine genuine antique beds with modern luxury mattresses and linen along with tea making facilities, televisions, DVD players, hairdryers and bathrobes to guarantee guest's absolute comfort.

The Hosts

Originally a teacher, Marion ran a restaurant and outside catering company before raising children took over and then managed the BAE VIP guest house which set the standards that were brought to St Mary's Mount. Together with Gerry, who is an engineer working in the oil and gas field, they ran a wine shop in Ulverston for many years and share a passion for food which is evident in the substantial breakfasts guests enjoy which include home-made jams and marmalades, plus eggs from their own hens. Both enjoy fell walking and share their knowledge to help their guests enjoy the beauty of the area to the full.

The Location

St Mary's Mount is in a quiet area of Ulverston, a pleasant market town on the edge of the Lake District National Park and one hour's drive from the Yorkshire Dales. Ulverston is world-renowned for its many festivals that offer something for everyone and the many National Trust attractions, fell walking and lakes provide a varied and exciting holiday.

Finding Us

Take J36 from M6, follow A590 to Barrow, when reaching Ulverston at second roundabout turn right to town centre, follow road around to junction, turn very sharp right, follow road up around to left past church, follow road around to right, take first turning on left signed Hoad Monument. St Mary's Mount drive is on right.

Rooms (per person per night incl. breakfast)

1 King Size (5') Room	(en suite)	£45
1 Double (4'6") Room	(en suite)	£45
1 Twin (2 x 3') Room	(private)	£45
1 Single (3') Room	(private)	£45
Single Occupancy		£50

Meals

Supper	£20
Dinner	£27.50

Opening Times

Closed Christmas & New Year

Payment Options

Facilities & Services

The Property

Johnby Hall is a great location from which to explore all that the Lake District has to offer. Steeped in history, the Elizabethan manor house started life around 1350 as a fortified pele tower and has belonged to the Howard family since 1783. It is now home to Henry and Anna Howard who welcome guests looking for a comfortable base from which to enjoy the surrounding area.

Located in a pretty cottage in the garden, the Studio is an open-plan suite offering superbly comfortable double or twin accommodation; an extra occasional bed in the sitting-room area makes this a great option for families. (A cot and cot bed are also available.) Kelly is in a seventeenth-century wing of the house and offers twin or double arrangements, with its own delightful sitting room. Breakfast is taken in the stunning 'great hall' where the history of the house is evident all around you, from family coats of arms to antique oak furniture and carefully-preserved architectural features.

Guests will meet the free range chickens and rare breed pigs, and can explore the extensive gardens and woodlands which are full of wildlife including red squirrels and deer.

The Hosts

Henry and Anna are both part-time professional musicians – Henry is a tenor and Anna is a harpist and soprano. (Musical guests feel especially at home here, and can enjoy playing the pianos in the Studio and great hall.) Henry, Anna and their young family are dedicated to ensuring a warm and friendly welcome for their guests.

The Location

Johnby Hall is located near Penrith in Cumbria, with the Lake District National Park's fells, dales and lakes on the doorstep. Guests will enjoy the many tourist attractions such as lake steamers, historic houses, gardens, castles and the many events, craft fairs and festivals that take place locally throughout the year in this part of Cumbria.

Henry and Anna Howard
Johnby Hall
Penrith
Cumbria CA11 0UU
Tel: 017684 83257 or 017684 80247
bookings@johnbyhall.co.uk
www.johnbyhall.co.uk   8955

Finding Us

Leave M6 at Penrith, J40. Take A66 westbound towards Keswick. After couple miles (and a little after Rheged roundabout) take right exit marked Greystoke. At next T junction turn left to Greystoke (B5288). At Greystoke village green turn right to Johnby taking left fork at Cycle Cafe. Johnby Hall is on left with white gates after a mile. Do not follow Sat Nav.

Rooms (per person per night incl. breakfast)

2 King Size (5') & Single (3') Suites (en suite)	**£62.50**
Single Supplement	**£25**

Meals

Supper – by prior arrangement	**£20**

Opening Times

Open all year

Payment Options

Facilities & Services

Mrs Lucy Sclater
Cook House
Church Road
Levens, Kendal
Cumbria LA8 8PU
Tel: 01539 561425
lucy@sclater.co.uk
www.sclater.co.uk   8958

The Property

Cook House is situated in the historic Cumbrian village of Levens overlooking Morecambe Bay and the Kent estuary, which together form a dramatically changing backdrop to this most beautiful home. As its name implies, the house was formerly a cook house for weary travellers making their way across the valley. Charmingly typical of this beautiful area, Cook House is perfectly located for exploring the southern lakes as well as a convenient stop off on the way to Scotland.

You'll be welcomed on arrival with afternoon tea in the conservatory, garden terrace or when the weather is inclement, beside a cosy fire in the drawing room. Lucy has made this house into a most comfortable home that is light and sunny and furnished with fine art, furniture and family photographs.

The bedrooms are very comfortable and offer every luxury for guests, one has an adjoining spacious modern bathroom, the other an en suite . Both overlook a rose and box garden, which is just one part of the pretty gardens surrounding Cook House, all of which have been designed by Lucy.

The Hosts

Lucy grew up in the nearby family home of Levens Hall which is now owned by her brother. Generations of talented family artists precede Lucy and she herself is a talented water-colourist, professional photographer and flower arranger and is locally recognised for her garden designing.

The Location

Levens is a pretty village just 4 miles from Kendal. Close by and open to the visitors is the Elizabethan family home of Levens Hall with its worldwide famous topiary garden. Sizergh Castle, Holker Hall and Leighton Hall are all close by. The damson blossom in the Lyth Valley in Spring is worth a visit, and of course the delights of the Lake District are on the doorstep.

Finding Us

M6 Junction 36. A590 dual carriageway to Kendal/The Lakes, 1st turn signed Barrow/The Lakes. Dual Carriageway for 1 mile take right turn signed Brigsteer & Levens Village. Right again in front of Hare & Hounds pub into Church Road. At top of hill are 2 signs for school & 20mph on right hand side, straight after signs is Cook House, name is on gate.

Rooms (per person per night incl. breakfast)

1 King Size (5') Room	(private)	£48
1 Twin (2 x 3') Room	(en suite)	£48
Single Occupancy		£55

10% discount for 3 nights or more
15% discount for 5 nights or more

Meals

Dinner	£30

Opening Times

Closed Christmas & New Year

Payment Options

Facilities & Services

The Property

Broomlands is the ideal base for visiting the Lake District National Park. This delightful Victorian house with magnificent views of the surrounding mountains, nestles in the Vale of Lorton, a relatively undiscovered valley situated between Cockermouth and Buttermere.

With Alison's keen eye for detail and a careful balance of original Victorian features blended with antiques, bold colour schemes and contemporary touches this lovingly restored home offers a truly warm welcome.

Log fires in winter or an airy garden room or outdoor terrace in warmer weather, provide the perfect setting to appreciate afternoon tea on arrival, with delicious homemade cake. Bernard's breakfasts include locally sourced ingredients like traditional Cumberland sausage and black pudding or perhaps smoked salmon and scrambled free range eggs.

All three bedrooms have individually designed en suite bathrooms (one with romantic double-ended slipper bath), king size beds, luxury bedding, towels, bathrobes and slippers, as well as indulgent toiletries.

The one acre garden is separated into 'rooms', each well established and with ample seating areas for guests to enjoy the stunning scenery and views, which change with the light as the day progresses. Secure storage is available for bicycles.

The Hosts

Alison and Bernard both ran their own businesses but are now semi-retired. Sharing a passion for fell walking, Bernard enjoys mountain biking and fell running, while Alison has her own horse and is a keen rider. Bernard is the chef and they both love entertaining their guests, delighting in meeting new people and sharing with them their thorough knowledge of the local area, walking and cycle routes. They are happy to provide packed lunches on request.

The Location

Broomlands is located 4 miles south of the market town of Cockermouth and six miles north of Buttermere and boasts five lakes within eight miles – ideal for B&B guests to enjoy spectacular scenery and unspoilt landscapes.

Bernard & Alison Moore
Broomlands, High Lorton,
Cockermouth, Cumbria CA13 9UL
Tel: 01900 85086
broomlandslakedistrict@gmail.com   8944
www.broomlandslakedistrict.co.uk

Finding Us

From Keswick continue on the A66 for a further mile, take left turn signed "Lorton via Whinlatter Pass". Follow B5292 for 6 miles. After the Lorton village sign continue for ½ mile, turn left, signed Buttermere. Lef again at bottom of hill, still following the signs to Buttermere. Continue for 1 mile keeping the continuous wall on your right. When you can read the signpost "Hopebec 1 mile", Broomlands will be on your left, immediately after Broomlands Barn.

Rooms (per person per night incl. breakfast)

1 Superior King Size (5') Room (en suite)	**£85**
2 King Size (5') Rooms (en suite)	**£65**
Single Occupancy	**£115-£155**

Minimum 2 night stay at weekends.

Meals

Dinner (3 courses)	**£32**
(By prior arrangement)	

Opening Times

Closed Christmas & New Year

Payment Options

Facilities & Services

The Property

Approaching Snelston along a narrow lane you catch glimpses through the trees of the idyllic parkland and pasture valley which surrounds this classic estate village.

Wrapped in climbing roses and wisteria, this is a listed brick building with lovely sandstone mullioned windows, leaded lights and striking chimneys. Family portraits and porcelain adorn the comfortable drawing room, elegant dining room and cosy library. There are two beautifully decorated and classically furnished bedrooms, each with original Victorian fireplaces. The bathrooms, one with a lovely view of the garden, have large cast iron baths to wallow in, excellent showers and all the accessories you need.

The serene one acre garden is a delight. Wander beyond deep herbaceous borders along grassy paths to a brook and a spring woodland garden planted with wood anemones, hellebores, narcissus, bluebells and fox gloves.

The Hosts

Your delightful hosts are Sue and Edmund Jarvis who receive all their guests with a warm hearted welcome, along with the vociferous but friendly Labrador. Sue, a Cordon Bleu cook, is down to earth, cheerful and meeting people gives her enormous pleasure. Edmund was a tea planter in India for five years before returning to a career in exports taking him to forty countries. These days he's often found in the garden with a wheelbarrow or sitting on a lawnmower.

The Location

Oldfield House close to Ashbourne, is perfectly situated for exploring the beautiful Derbyshire Dales, the Peak District National Park and for visiting great houses nearby including Chatsworth, Kedleston, Haddon, Hardwick, Calke Abbey, Sudbury and Melbourne Hall. Uttoxeter Racecourse is about 20 minutes away. Fly fishing is available on the Dove.

Edmund & Sue Jarvis
Oldfield House
Snelston
Ashbourne
Derbyshire DE6 2EP
01335 324510 or 07912 614807
sue_jarvis@talktalk.net
www.oldfieldhouse.uk.com   7992

Finding Us

From Ashbourne take A515 towards Lichfield and after about 3 miles turn right on a bend at sign for Snelston. Follow road 1¼ miles to centre of village, passing a gate lodge and church on right and red telephone kiosk on left. The house is opposite the stone cross. Turn right here and first left to rear of house.

Rooms (per person per night incl. breakfast)

1 King Size (5′) Room	(en suite)	**£50**
1 Twin (2 x 3′) Room	(private)	**£50**
Single Supplement		**£20**

Meals

Dinner	**£35**

Opening Times

Closed Christmas & New Year

Payment Options

Facilities & Services

Adrian Cunningham
Glendon House
7 Knowleston Place
Matlock
Derbyshire DE4 3BU
Tel: 01629 584732
contact@glendonbandb.co.uk
www.glendonbandb.co.uk   7971

Finding Us
Detailed directions available on request.

Rooms (per person per night incl. breakfast)

1 King Size (5') Four Poster Room (en suite)	**£47.50**
2 Super King (6')/Twin Rooms (en suite)	**£37.50**
1 King Size (5') Room (en suite)	**£37.50**
1 Family Double (4'6") & bunks (en suite)	**£37.50**
Single Occupancy	**£60**

Meals
Breakfast only

Opening Times
Open all year

Payment Options

Facilities & Services

The Property

An elegant Grade II listed Victorian house in the heart of Matlock in Derbyshire, the perfect base for visitors to the Peak District National Park.

On arrival guests receive a warm welcome and a delicious afternoon tea. This fabulous quintessentially English home has been sympathetically restored and furnished in a relaxed and stylish fashion. An attractive first floor sitting room with garden views provides an excellent haven and even offers a 'book swap'. Off-street parking is available.

Well appointed bedrooms, each individually furnished, one with a four poster bed, another a family room, all offer a range of facilities including flat screen televisions, ipod docking station and the highest quality bed and bath linens.

Breakfasts here are very special, served in a bright and airy room overlooking the lovely front garden, with everything freshly cooked to order. A full English is just one of the varied options available as well as cereals, fruits, yogurts and breads.

The Host

A fairly recent resident of Matlock, Adrian, a registered nurse and former teacher in the NHS, has known and loved the area far longer. Enjoying the countryside is combined with a fascination for history and enthusiasm for gardening plus a keen respect for the environment. Nothing is too much trouble, from providing early breakfasts for guests who are keen walkers and travellers, to making dinner reservations at the many very popular local restaurants and hostelries.

The Location

The glorious former spa town of Matlock's fascinating history and splendid surroundings are reason enough to visit. As well as outstanding natural beauty, the Peak District offers a plethora of family days out, museums, theme parks, stately homes and even a cable car. Much beckons too for the outdoor enthusiast, including cycling, walks and village trails.

Photograph: Clive Boursnell ©

The Property

Proudly overlooking the Otter Valley and Honiton, in what Daniel Defoe once called "the finest landscape in the world", rises Woodhayes, an elegant listed Georgian farmhouse.

Dating back to the 14th century, Woodhayes is steeped in history and has a fascinating literary connection. Noel's Page-Turner ancestor was great aunt to one of Britain's greatest ever writers, Jane Austen, who often frequented nearby Lyme Regis.

The antique furniture, luxurious beds with fine bed linen and walls adorned with original paintings (including full length family portraits) make this an impressive, yet comfortable home from home.

Guests are encouraged to explore the one and a half acre garden and scenic walks on the farm in this designated Area of Outstanding Natural Beauty. Local attractions such as Dumpdon Hill, a Celtic hill fort and Luppitt Church are also worth a visit.

The Hosts

Christy and Noel are passionate about good food and they delight in sharing delicious four course meals, featuring the finest home grown vegetables and local meat and fish, with their guests. Active members of the local community, they clearly enjoy entertaining and meeting people from all walks of life. Noel can often be found mowing, planting trees, pruning the topiary and he also spends a lot of time involved with voluntary organisations.

The Location

The Jurassic Coast (including the fossil hunter's paradise of Lyme Regis), East Devon and Dorset are on the doorstep as is Honiton, the 'antique capital' of the South West with its bi-annual arts and music festival and the world's premier collection of Honiton lace.

Noel and Christy Page-Turner
Woodhayes
Honiton, Devon EX14 4TP
Tel: 01404 42011
Fax: 01404 42011
cmpt@inweb.co.uk
www.woodhayes.co.uk   2997

Finding Us

Woodhayes is situated 1½ miles north east of Honiton. Take Dunkeswell road out of Honiton, cross small bridge over River Otter. 150 yards turn right. Woodhayes is first drive on left.

Rooms (per person per night incl. breakfast)

1 Single (3') Room	(private)	**£46**
1 King Size (5') Room	(en suite)	**£48**
1 Twin (2 x 3') Room	(en suite)	**£48**
Single Occupancy of Double or Twin		**£56**

Meals

Dinner	**£30**

Opening Times

Closed occasionally

Payment Options

Facilities & Services

David & Helen Littlefair
Stoke Gabriel Lodgings
Badgers Retreat
2 Orchard Close
Paignton Road
Stoke Gabriel
Totnes
Devon TQ9 6SX
Tel: 01803 782003 or 07785 710225
Fax: 01803 782003
info@stokegabriellodgings.com   **2959**

Finding Us

Detailed instructions available at time of booking.

Rooms (per person per night incl. breakfast)

2 King Size (5') Rooms (en suite)	£45-£50
1 Super King (6') /Twin Room (en suite)	£45-£50
Single Supplement	£25

Meals

Breakfast Only

Opening Times

Closed Christmas

Payment Options

Facilities & Services

The Property

Stunning modern architecture, bright open living spaces and incredible views are the hallmarks of Stoke Gabriel Lodgings. Set high above the River Dart just outside the quintessentially English village of Stoke Gabriel, the house was completed in 2010 and has been designed to take full advantage of its elevated location deep in the Devon countryside.

On arrival you will be warmly greeted by your hosts David and Helen and offered a classic Devon cream tea and a chance to take in your rather special surroundings. The guest rooms are spacious and luxuriously furnished with comfortable seating areas, televisions and delicious offerings on tea trays. The en suite bathrooms are equally well thought out and designed complete with wet shower areas and heated towel rails for added comfort. Patio doors open to your own private balcony overlooking the garden – a perfectly quiet retreat to enjoy the peaceful location.

Oak floors, and furniture of the guest living and dining rooms reflect the contemporary light and airy ambience whilst outside the newly planted garden landscape is best enjoyed from the large terrace or conservatory. Breakfast offers an array of cooked delights whilst dinner can be taken at one of the many excellent local pubs and restaurants.

The Hosts

As hoteliers for over 30 years, David and Helen Littlefair know exactly what their guests expect and, together with their three grown-up daughters have created a lovely family home to share. Holidaying in Stoke Gabriel for many years before building a home here, their intimate knowledge of the best places to visit are eagerly shared with their guests.

The Location

National Trust and English Heritage properties as well as the South Devon Coastal Path, beaches galore and the diversely interesting towns of Brixham, Dartmouth, Totnes, Paignton and Torquay are all within reach. Above all take in the wild open splendour of Dartmoor for walking and cycling.

Sue & Guy Sherratt
Bracken House, Bratton Fleming,
Barnstaple, Devon EX31 4TG
Tel: 01598 711810
info@brackenhouse.co.uk
www.brackenhouse.co.uk   **2961**

The Property

A short distance from the centre of the pretty Devon village of Bratton Fleming, amidst seven acres of gardens is the old rectory known as Bracken House. Home to Sue and Guy Sherratt, and their two children since 2009 it is now a welcoming family home. Antiques and art sit comfortably alongside relaxed furnishings and the library is packed with interesting books. A Devon cream tea on arrival is served in the library or on fine days outside on the plant-filled terrace.

Bracken House was once home to Reverend Wodehouse, uncle of PG Wodehouse who is known to have stayed here, perhaps drawing inspiration for some of his colourful characters. The guest rooms are suitably named 'Jeeves', 'Wooster' and 'Anatole'. 'Jeeves' has a double bed, 'Wooster' can be either a twin or a double and 'Anatole' is the 4'6" double on the ground floor and all three have en suites furnished with the finishing touches you would expect. Delicious breakfasts, and a supper if you choose, feature local produce and seasonal offerings from the garden.

Outside the wonderful views across the surrounding countryside extend across Devon and on clear days to the sea and across to Clovelly and Hartland Point.

The Hosts

Sue is a professional harpist and when not gardening, riding or looking after her guests, finds time to play concerts and teach. Guy is a chartered surveyor with his own estate agency with properties in France, Spain and Florida. In his spare time he enjoys cooking and gardening.

The Location

Bracken House is located in Bratton Fleming, near Barnstaple in Devon and is the perfect base for exploring all of Exmoor and Devon with their many varied beaches, pretty villages and towns such as Croyde, Dunster, Barnstaple, South Molton and Ilfracombe. Lundy Island and Woolacombe Bay are all within reach and easy access to A361 takes you down into Cornwall too.

Finding Us

From South Molton, take A399 towards Ilfracombe; continue on road past Brayford continue until left turning towards Bratton Fleming. Bear left into village. Downhill for 500 yards and, opposite Post Office, turn left down drive with a sign at the end and follow signs down to the house.

Rooms (per person per night incl. breakfast)

1 King Size (5') Room (en suite)	**£47.50-£52.50**
1 Super King (6')/Twin Room (en suite)	**£45-£50**
1 Double (4'6") Room (en suite)	**£42.50-£47.50**
Single Supplement	**£25**

Meals

Supper (By prior arrangement)	from **£20**

Opening Times

Open all year

Payment Options

Facilities & Services

The Property

An ultimate luxury boutique Wolsey Lodge – and more! Personally guided tours of Dartmoor, accommodation in a divine secluded Devon Longhouse overlooking surrounding hills; dining on the finest local fare and the care of truly kind and caring hosts – what more could you want?

Located just outside the village of Cornworthy near the River Dart, the original Kerswell farmhouse dates back 400 years. Additions and refurbishment allow it to offer all modern-day luxuries for an extremely comfortable stay. There are five well appointed bedrooms, three in the main house and two in the adjacent barn conversion. Rooms have under floor heating, sumptuous pocket-sprung mattresses, goose down duvets, are individually styled and finishing touches including fresh flowers, well-stocked tea trays and White Company toiletries.

The house is very comfortable, airy and light with plentiful reading materials, local maps and guides to assist your stay.

The Hosts

Graham and Nichola Hawkins will welcome you at Kerswell. Graham ran an international school in Kuwait for 17 years and Nichola was an interior designer before returning to Devon. Nichola, a most accomplished cook, prepares a fine repertoire of local Devon fayre to tempt her guests.

The Location

The gardens and grounds around this luxury boutique Wolsey Lodge may dissuade you from venturing further, but Dartmoor is on your doorstep and also the South Devon Coast Path, South Hams AONB, Dartmouth with its lovely harbour, the ancient town of Totnes and Ashburton with its antiques centre.   Blue Flag beaches, steam railways, historic houses, castles and gardens aplenty are also nearby.

Graham & Nichola Hawkins
Kerswell Farmhouse
Cornworthy, Totnes, Devon TQ9 7HH
Tel: 01803 732013
gjnhawkins@rocketmail.com
www.kerswellfarmhouse.co.uk   2955

Finding Us

From M5/A38 to Plymouth - Exit Dart Bridge Junction A384 to Totnes - At roundabout in Dartington left A385 - At lights in Totnes right A381 to Kingsbridge - At top of hill left to Ashprington - At first crossroads left between pillars - At second crossroads right to Bow Bridge, follow road to Tuckenhay - At T-junction follow road left - At top of hill right to Tideford and Dartmouth - Kerswell Farmhouse is on the right after Furze Cross.

Rooms   (per person per night incl. breakfast)

1 Super King (6')/Twin Room with Sitting Room (en suite)	**£70**
2 Super King (6') /Twin Rooms (en suite)	**£60**
2 King Size (5') Rooms (en suite)	**£55-£60**

Single Occupancy – 75% of room rate (Non-Bank Holiday Sun-Thurs only)

Meals

Breakfast only

Opening Times

Closed December and New Year's Day

Payment Options

£ C TC

Facilities & Services

Emma & Chuck Guest
Glebe House
Southleigh
Colyton
Devon
EX24 6SD
Tel: 01404 871276 or 07867 568569
emma_guest@talktalk.net
www.guestsatglebe.com   2951

The Property

Nestling in the unspoilt, lovely and relatively unknown Coly Valley in the heart of East Devon is the home of the aptly named Guest family who offer the warmest of welcomes to their guests. At the end of a sweeping drive and surrounded by mature gardens with panoramic views of the gorgeous landscape and its own 15 acres, this Wolsey Lodge also offers use of a the outdoor heated swimming pool and tennis court.

The house itself is furnished with interesting pictures, paintings and momentos gleaned while travelling the world. Visitors can use the elegant drawing room with garden views or the cosy upstairs sitting/television room and the lovely conservatory with its ancient vine.

There are three comfortable, classically furnished and elegant bedrooms, all with en suite bathrooms, one being a family room.

The Hosts

Both have extensive hospitality experience and it shows. They share a love of good food and wine and Emma is an excellent chef having catered professionally for many years. They met while working on yachts and Chuck is a master mariner with extensive experience captaining super yachts. As their three sons have now left home they decided to make Glebe House a bed and breakfast as chartering ashore would be fun!

The Location

The Coly valley is one of the main tributary valleys of the River Axe in East Devon. It is the ideal place to relax and unwind, yet is well placed for visiting the Jurassic Coast, the Coastal Path through the old fishing and smuggling towns of Beer and Branscombe, Honiton with its antiques and markets, or the cathedral city of Exeter. There is much to do and see for families, walkers or those wanting a more cultural break. For visitors en route to Cornwall it is a delightful spot for an overnight stay but it is even better for the perfect country weekend escape.

Finding Us

Detailed directions available on request.

Rooms

(per person per night incl. breakfast)

1 Double (4'6") Room (en suite)	**£40**
1 Twin (2 x 3') Room (en suite)	**£40**
1 Family Room with King Size (5') & Twin (2 x 3') (en suite)	**£40**
plus £20 for one child (and £15 for second child)	
Single Supplement	**£10**

Meals

Supper (2 Courses)	**£20**
Dinner (3 Courses)	**£25**
(Both by prior arrangement)	

Opening Times

Closed Christmas & New Year

Payment Options

Facilities & Services

Stuart Litster & Kevin Hooper
Strete Barton House
Totnes Road
Strete
Dartmouth
Devon TQ6 0RU
Tel: 01803 770364
info@stretebarton.co.uk
www.stretebarton.co.uk   2950

Finding Us

Detailed directions available on request.

Rooms (per person per night incl. breakfast)

2 Super King (6') Rooms (en suite)	£58-£80
1 Super King (6') /Twin Room (en suite)	£53-£58
2 King Size (5') Rooms (en suite)	£58-£63
1 King Size (5') Room (private)	£58-£63

Surcharge will apply for Dartmouth Regatta & Christmas season.

Meals

Breakfast only

Opening Times

Closed New Year

Payment Options

Facilities & Services

The Property

Described as 'Stretes ahead' this 16th Century luxury manor house is perfect for exploring the glorious Dartmouth area. With extensive grounds and panoramic sea views across Start Bay and the headland, visitors approach through an immaculate walled garden.

The house was extensively yet sympathetically renovated by Stuart and Kevin, whose warm welcome and attention to detail encourage repeat visits. Contemporary, designer furnishings, Asian artefacts collected during their travels and stylish touches combine for a distinctive rural retreat. The inviting sitting room with a real fire is the ideal place to unwind with a book taken from their library.

Six generously proportioned bedrooms, including one suite, some with sea views, are all beautifully decorated. Five have en suite and one a private bathroom. Large beds, fine linens, luxury mattresses, down pillows and a hospitality tray are standard, plus indulgent toiletries. A clothes/boot drying room is an extra consideration if required.

The Hosts

Stuart and Kevin moved here seven years ago, having both worked in London. A long-standing dream to run a luxury bed and breakfast was realised when this gorgeous house came on the market. Kevin still works a few days each week in Chambers in London, while Stuart looks after guests. They love this area, provide extensive information packs of local information in their bedrooms and are pleased to recommend and book local restaurants, some just a short stroll from the house.

The Location

Five miles from multi-cultural Dartmouth, handy for sailing at Salcombe or visiting Kingsbridge, this is ideally situated for exploring the South Hams area and beaches. For walkers, the South West Coast Path is just 30 metres away and golfing clients are offered a discount at the Dartmouth Golf & Country Club. Many regattas and festivals, including food, music and The International Festival of Worm Charming take place locally.

Nicky Robbins & James Wortley
Ashley House
3 Paradise Lawn, South Molton
Devon EX36 3DJ   **2946**
Tel: 01769 573444 or 07816 776727
info@ashleyhousebedandbreakfast.com
www.ashleyhousebedandbreakfast.com

Finding Us

Leave M5 at J27, at roundabout take exit to A361 Tiverton/Barnstaple. At next roundabout take 2nd exit continue on A361. At next roundabout take 1st exit onto B3227 South Molton. Continue until Murco Garage on left. Just past this is Paradise Lawn behind black wrought iron railings, on the right, opposite Simmons shop. Ashley House is at the back of Paradise Lawn. Parking instructions will be sent with confirmation.

The Property

Ashley House is situated in the heart of the lovely historic Devon market town of South Molton. Set in the picturesque conservation area of Paradise Lawn it is a substantial semi-detached Victorian home with an intriguing history and is featured on the official South Molton Heritage Trail.

Beautifully restored keeping many original features, and stylishly furnished with a clever mix of antique and contemporary furniture, everything is top quality. Guests have a separate dining/sitting room with wood burning stove and leather sofa. Bedrooms, all with en suite shower rooms, are equipped with Egyptian cotton linen and white fluffy towels, locally produced toiletries, hospitality tray with fresh milk and mineral water, television and Wi-Fi. Ashley House is a showcase for this gorgeous area, with stacks of information for guests and fabulous framed photographs by an acclaimed local photographer. It also offers secure parking for guests.

The Hosts

Nicky has spent many years in the film business. Her partner Jamie runs a communications agency for the travel industry. Nothing is too much trouble for their guests and they are happy to recommend local pubs and restaurants, make reservations and book taxis. Breakfasts are excellent with eggs from their hens, locally sourced bacon and sausages, homemade preserves and home grown fruit and vegetables.

The Location

There's much for everyone to see and do in this fabulous area. Stroll around this busy market town with its pannier market, local independent shops, museum, honey farm and chocolate factory, or head for the superb North Devon beaches. South Molton is the gateway to Exmoor National Park and well placed to visit historic houses and beautiful gardens. South Molton is the perfect place to explore this stunning area.

Rooms (per person per night incl. breakfast)

1 King Size (5') Room (en suite)   **£45-£60**

2 Double (4'6") Rooms   **£35-£50**
(en suite)

Single occupancy £10 less than full room rate.

Meals

Breakfast only

Opening Times

Open all year

Payment Options

Facilities & Services

Carolyn & Michael Jones
Straightway Head House,
Whimple, Exeter,
Devon EX5 2QS
Tel: 01404 822177 or 07894 575975
contact@straightwayheadhouse.co.uk
www.straightwayheadhouse.co.uk 2944

Finding Us

From A30 travelling west, 6 miles after
Honiton turn off at Daisymount exit signed
Exmouth, Budleigh Salterton & Ottery St.
Mary. Turn right at first roundabout signed
Whimple. At second roundabout go
straight, signed Whimple. After ¼ mile turn
right signed Straightway Head, Fairmile
and Larkbeare. After ½ mile turn left signed
Larkbeare. Straightway Head House is first
house on right.

The Property

Straightway Head House was built in the early 1930's in
the Arts & Crafts style and sympathetically extended. The
resulting light and spacious house on the edge of the village
of Whimple has stunning views across Dartmoor and guests
can enjoy spectacular sunsets from the terrace. Antiques
mixed with contemporary furnishings; woodburning stove
in cold weather; a well-stocked library - plus a warm
welcome - await. A magnificent Devon cream tea is served
on arrival.

The large, airy bedrooms are all en suite and beautifully
furnished – again a mix of contemporary and antique with
fine linens, comfortable beds, and televisions and DVD's.
The addition of fresh flowers and a jar of homemade
cookies are typical of the attention to detail here.

Guests enjoy delicious and generous breakfasts served
in the dining room (with log fire in colder months) or in
the conservatory with garden views. Carefully and locally
sourced ingredients are included, as well as Carolyn's
legendary homemade bread and preserves.

The Hosts

Carolyn, a Cordon Bleu cook, has cooked on yachts, in
directors' dining rooms and also taught cookery in France.
An accomplished violinist, she collects art, antiques and
books. Her delicious dinners are very popular but she is
also happy to recommend the many excellent restaurants
and pubs nearby. Mike, also an excellent cook, is an
accountant, a keen walker and marathon runner and
pleased to recommend scenic routes to enjoy the locality.

The Location

Situated in an area of Outstanding Natural Beauty, between
Honiton and Exeter and within easy reach of the A30, there
is something near here for all ages and tastes. Exeter brims
with history and heritage, Dartmoor and Exmoor National
Parks are in easy reach, as are stately homes, museums,
castles, gardens, sporting activities, balloon rides, interesting
shops, seaside resorts and deserted beaches.

Rooms (per person per night incl. breakfast)

1 Super King (6')/Twin Room (en suite)	£55
1 King Size (5') Room (en suite)	£50
1 Round Single (4'6") Room (en suite)	£70
Single Supplement	£20

Meals

Supper (2 courses)	£25
Dinner (3 courses)	£35

Opening Times

Open all year

Payment Options

£ € C TC PayPal

Facilities & Services

BYO C 🏠 🐾 ⬆️ ♿
WiFi 🚭

Mrs Hilary Tucker
Beera Farmhouse, Milton Abbot
Tavistock, Devon PL19 8PL
Tel: 01822 870216 or 07974 957966
Hilary@beera-farm.co.uk
www.beera-farm.co.uk   2942

Finding Us

From Okehampton on A386 via Tavistock. At Tavistock, at 1st mini roundabout take first exit, at 2nd mini roundabout take last exit (signed town centre), at 3rd roundabout go left, at 4th roundabout go right, at the next roundabout (Spar shop ahead) go right, then approx 200 yards take sharp left up hill, signed Hospital & Lamerton. Continue for 5½ miles. On entering Milton Abbot take first left signed Endsleigh Gardens, go down road for 2.2 miles, farm is on left.

The Property

This imposing Victorian farmhouse was built in 1856 by the Duke of Bedford and has views of the Tamar Valley and rolling Devon countryside.

With gardens (complete with 'ha ha') surrounded by their own farmland and grazing livestock, there are orchards, picnic tables, swing and slide for children to enjoy. This is a real Devon delight according to guests.

Inside, many original features remain, and this comfortable family home has a guest sitting room, with television and DVD player, wood burning stove, piano, local information, maps and reading material. On arrival, experience a traditional cream tea here, or in the garden.

Legendary farmhouse breakfasts with homemade preserves, and dinners (by prior arrangement) will feature home reared meats and locally grown produce.

Light and airy bedrooms (one with four poster) all en suite, have great showers and contemporary furnishings, offering everything guests might want (including homemade biscuits and local fudge on the hospitality tray!).

The Hosts

Robert grew up on this farm and Hilary, too, is from a local farming family. A professionally trained chef, she produces excellent breakfasts and evening meals and, with sufficient notice, even packed lunches. The Tuckers have three young sons who enjoy meeting guests. Families staying on the farm love to watch the lambs and the farm in action. Very involved in their community, Robert and Hilary are fonts of local knowledge and always happy to book local restaurants and hostelries.

The Location

Located in the parish of Milton Abbot, near Tavistock and situated on the border of Devon and Cornwall in a designated Area of Outstanding Natural Beauty. Everything for a family day out including numerous National Trust properties, beaches, moors, coastal walks, gardens, cycle routes, museums and glorious tea rooms and pubs await.

Rooms (per person per night incl. breakfast)

1 Super King (6') /Twin Room (en suite)	**£40-£46**
1 King Size (5') Four Poster Room (en suite)	**£40-£46**
1 King Size (5') Room (en suite)	**£40-£46**
Single Occupancy	**£60-£65**

Meals

Supper (2 courses)	**£20**
Dinner (3 courses)	**£25**
(Both by prior arrangement)	

Opening Times

Closed during lambing - 3 weeks from end of February usually.

Payment Options

Facilities & Services

Tim & Victoria Cunningham
Burnville House
Brentor
Tavistock
Devon PL19 0NE
Tel: 01822 820443 or 07881 583471
burnvillef@aol.com
www.burnville.co.uk   2943

Finding Us
A30 Exeter-Okehampton; A386 towards Tavistock. Right for Lydford opposite Dartmoor Inn. After 4 miles through village of Lydford, Burnville Farm on left (convex traffic mirror on right).

The Property
Arrive at this elegant Georgian farmhouse through listed granite gateposts and along the winding drive. Burnville House is on a working farm in Devon, between the villages of Lydford and Brentor, near Tavistock, part of the Dartmoor National Park. Lawns and wildflower carpeted woods, with views over Dartmoor entice guests to relax and appreciate the splendid vista.

A large hall and sweeping staircase lead to the generously proportioned and classically decorated bedrooms with en suite bath/shower rooms. There are hidden fridges and antique furniture cleverly mixed with the contemporary. Entertainment systems, luxurious bathrooms, toiletries, linens, fresh flowers and hospitality trays offer understated luxury and style. A tennis court and heated swimming pool plus a games room complete with skittles, are also available for guests to enjoy.

Remarkably good breakfasts are served in the dining room, where guests also enjoy fabulous dinners, by prior arrangement. Produce from the farm and locally sourced ingredients are used where possible.

The Hosts
Tim and Victoria upped sticks from careers in London to farm and raise their family in Devon. The 250 acre organic farm has sheep (guests are welcome to help feed the lambs) and suckler cows. Victoria, a very accomplished cook, and Tim enjoy an outdoor life, riding, cycling, tennis, shooting and sailing when they have spare time. Their exceptional hospitality skills result in a high proportion of return visitors, so early booking is advisable.

The Location
Outdoor enthusiasts are spoilt for choice here. Head east to explore Dartmoor by foot or mountain bike; drive south for the delights of Tavistock and the beauty of the Tamar Valley. Further on, explore fishing villages on the south coast and the cathedral city of Exeter. North is Cornwall's rugged coastline or venture west to The Eden Project and the Lost Gardens of Heligan. National Trust properties abound.

Rooms (per person per night incl. breakfast)
3 Super King (6') Rooms   **£42.50-£47.50** (en suite)
Single Supplement   **£15**

Meals
Dinner (3 courses)   **£27**

Opening Times
Open all year

Payment Options

Facilities & Services

John & Fleur Hoare
Huish Manor,
Winterborne Zelston, Blandford Forum,
Dorset DT11 9ES
Tel: 01929 459065
hoare@huish.fsnet.co.uk   **1995**

The Property

This very pretty, Grade II listed house, built in 1792, is approached along an attractive tree lined drive and is fronted by a large lawn with a pretty walled garden at the back and an adjoining small wood, orchard, and paddocks.

The house has attractive well proportioned rooms as befits a house of this period. The drawing room and dining room are available for guests' use and are furnished with antiques and a fine collection of marine paintings. The dining room is particularly elegant with a log fire, lit when appropriate, at both dinner and breakfast.

The bedrooms are large, with antique furniture and comfortable beds made up with linen sheets and warm blankets. Each has its own bathroom, one with a power shower, and enjoy calming views either onto the front lawn, or the walled garden at the back.

The Hosts

John worked in the City of London until retiring. He is a keen sailor. Fleur trained as a dancer and, until recently, taught children ballet. Fleur is an excellent cook and they both greatly enjoy entertaining guests in the surroundings of their attractive 18th century house.

The Location

The house is ideally situated for visiting Hardy Country including Dorchester, Blandford Forum, Wimborne, Studland Bay, and Poole. There are a number of interesting museums, beautiful houses such as Kingston Lacy and castles at Corfe and Lulworth. For those who enjoy walking, there is the lovely Dorset coastline, recently declared a World Heritage Site. Other attractions include the famous Dorset Steam Fair in August.

Finding Us

Travelling West on A31, past Wimborne, there is a 2 mile long brick wall on the left. At the end of this, and 50 yards past the Worlds End public house, there is a sign 'Huish only' indicating a slip road to the right, leading to the drive of the house. This is before the turning to Winterborne Zelston.

Rooms (per person per night incl. breakfast)

1 Double (4'6") Room (private)	**£45-£55**
1 Twin (2 x 3') Room (private)	**£45-£55**
Single Supplement	**£10**

Meals

Dinner   **£26**

Opening Times

Closed Christmas, New Year & Easter

Payment Options

Facilities & Services

Peter & Cari Sorby
Manor Barn
Upper Street,
Child Okeford,
Blandford Forum,
Dorset DT11 8EF
Tel: 01258 860638 or 07973 595344
carisorby@btinternet.com　　　　　**1986**
www.manorbarnbedandbreakfast.co.uk

Finding Us

Heading south on A350 from Shaftesbury, turn right at the sign 'Child Okeford 3 miles'. Nearly 3 miles later Manor Barn drive is on the left immediately in front of a 20mph road sign

The Property

Let's set the scene for a real treat; an old red brick and stone house, an area of outstanding natural beauty and a very caring hostess. Manor Barn offers all this ~ and more!

This beautifully converted barn has its own entrance into a sitting room with a private breakfast area and two very stylish ground floor, oak beamed bedrooms each with a stunning en suite bathroom. Cari is a wonderful hostess, offering tea and homemade cakes on arrival and the sort of breakfast that sets one up for a day spent exploring this lovely area, all produced using mostly local ingredients.

The ground floor bedrooms are ideal for less able guests and Cari excels at making sure their needs are met. From the front of the house is a spectacular view of Hambledon Hill and by following the footpath from the end of the drive to the top of the hill you will be rewarded with amazing views over five counties and the knowledge that you have achieved a climb of some 603 feet and therefore thoroughly deserve to relax in luxury on your return.

The Hosts

Cari and Peter are welcoming and charming hosts who look after guests as if they are old friends. Peter works in nearby Sherborne whilst Cari looks after the house, their two sons, and the family's dogs. They both love this area of Dorset and sharing their favourite places with guests.

The Location

Dorset is a wonderful county, boasting glorious coastline, beautiful countryside, pretty villages and market towns and some of the most archaeologically important sites in the country along the Jurassic coast. Sherborne with its castle and Abbey is close by and there are magnificent houses and gardens at Kingston Lacy, Athelhampton House, Longleat and Stourhead within easy reach.

Rooms (per person per night incl. breakfast)

2 Super King (6')/Twin Rooms (en suite)	**£55**
Single Supplement	**£25**

Meals
Breakfast only

Opening Times
Open all year

Payment Options

Facilities & Services

The Property

Arriving in Ashmore on a fine day one is able to appreciate just how high you've climbed with views across to the Dorset coast and the Isle of Wight over 30 miles away. Tear yourself away for tea and home baked cakes at Glebe Farm which is situated in the heart of the village. Built in 2004 and designed to take advantage of the magnificent views all around as well as the complete and utter tranquillity of this quiet slice of Dorset. Inside, glass walls create a light and spacious feel and the central dining hall with its completely glazed wall allows uninterrupted views across the fields beyond.

The bedrooms, located to the side of the house, are beautifully furnished with armchairs and table, well-stocked hospitality tray, fresh flowers, television, iPod docks and internet access. The upstairs room has a Juliette balcony whilst downstairs French doors lead on to a private deck to make the most of the views.

A light supper is offered for guests in their room if they choose or guests can enjoy a full dinner in the dining room or candlelit terrace. Whichever option is chosen, enjoy local fare supplemented by homemade produce all cooked to perfection and enjoyed in the most wonderful setting.

The Hosts

Tessa and Ian Millard oversaw the building of the house themselves before moving in from their farmhouse next door. They have three grown up children and run a large arable, sheep and beef farm. Dogs and horses are family favourites here and Tessa enjoys the additional challenge of side-saddle on one of her horses.

The Location

Ashmore has a dewpond dating back to Roman times which is not to be missed; neither are the many walks emanating from the village. Stonehenge, Shaftesbury, Salisbury, Stourhead House, Abbotsbury Swannery and the Jurassic coast are all within reach.

Tessa & Ian Millard
Glebe Farm
Ashmore
Shaftesbury
Dorset SP5 5AE
Tel: 01747 811974 or 07799858961
tmillard@glebe.f9.co.uk
www.glebefarmbandb.co.uk   1977

Finding Us

From Shaftesbury take A30 towards Salisbury. After 3 miles enter Ludwell. At top of hill turn right (signed Ashmore) follow road to top of hill. Left at crossroads. After 200yds turn right, follow road into Ashmore. Pass pond in centre of village. Just past memorial on right is Glebe Farm sign.

Rooms (per person per night incl. breakfast)

2 Super King (6') Rooms (en suite)	£50-£60
Single Supplement	£20

Meals

Supper	£15
Dinner	£25

(Both by prior arrangement)

Opening Times

Closed Christmas & New Year

Payment Options

Facilities & Services

Katie Pope
Wrackleford House
Dorchester
Dorset DT2 9SN
Tel: 01305 264141
katie@wrackleford.co.uk
www.wrackleford.co.uk   1976

Finding Us

Wrackleford House is set 2 miles north of the county town of Dorchester, close to the village of Stratton. Detailed directions available on request.

Rooms (per person per night incl. breakfast)

3 King Size (5') Rooms (en suite)	£70
1 Super King (6')/ Twin Room (en suite)	£70
Single Supplement	£40

Meals

Breakfast only

Opening Times

Closed Christmas & New Year

Payment Options

Facilities & Services

The Property

Staying on what is arguably one of the country's finest fishing and shooting estates is of course a treat for any sportsman. Combine this with a fine Georgian country house offering exceptionally luxurious B&B hospitality and you have a location anyone would be happy to visit.

The Wrackleford Estate has been in the Pope family for six generations and is now home to Katie and Oliver and their three children. Set in the heart of the Frome Valley in Dorset, everything here is gloriously and quintessentially English and the house is a classic reflection of this with antique furnishing, family photos and paintings, whilst outside the sweeping lawns lead down to the River Wrackle and beyond are meadows and a waterfall. A welcoming tea on arrival is enjoyed in the plant-filled conservatory whilst a sunny spot outside is the perfect location for a lazy breakfast.

Each guest room is large and comfortable with bathrooms that feature marble bath and basin surrounds and feel, quite simply, luxuriously decadent. Breakfast is an excellent affair of local produce and Katie will pack you a sumptuous picnic lunch or offer to cook a barbecue on the river banks if you're fishing. Dinner can be enjoyed at any of the excellent local restaurants. Bicycles are available on request.

The Hosts

Wrackleford is Oliver's family home but he spent time in the army before moving here with his young family in 2006. A keen interest in the countryside makes both he and Katie natural guardians of this wonderful estate and they enthusiastically and warmly welcome their B&B guests to enjoy all it has to offer with them.

The Location

Aside from the estate fishing and shooting, this area of Dorset has much to offer visitors. The Thomas Hardy and Tutankhamun museums, Maiden Castle, Cerne Abbas Giant, Corfe and Sherborne Castles, Longleat and the wild Jurassic coast are all within easy reach.

Dr and Mrs J Ireland
Aylworth Manor
Aylworth, Naunton
Gloucestershire GL54 3AH
Tel: 01451 850850 or 07768 810357
enquiries@aylworthmanor.co.uk
www.aylworthmanor.co.uk   5948

Finding Us

From A40 at Northleach take A429 towards Bourton-on-the-Water, after 100 yards turn left signed Turkdean & Notgrove. Follow road for 3.9 miles to 'T' junction, turn right, take first left signed Aylworth. After ¾ mile entrance to drive is signed Aylworth Manor. If you start to go up other side of hill you have gone too far.

The Property
Location, location, location. What a perfect place to find a Wolsey Lodge. Set in the heart of the glorious Cotswold hills you cannot help but appreciate the seclusion of Aylworth Manor and yet you are no more than 12 miles from the bustling, interesting heart of Cheltenham and less than an hour from Stratford-upon-Avon and Oxford.

Aylworth Manor is over 500 years old and has been carefully restored over the last few years by John and Joanna Ireland who together have turned it into a most friendly, welcoming family home for their two children and the many guests that are lucky to discover them. Tea and homemade cakes mark your arrival before you are shown around the house and to your lovely, spacious room. There are three guest rooms, each with wonderful far-reaching views over the garden, farmland and valley beyond.

Outside, the gardens extend around the house where you will find spring-fed ponds, greatly enjoyed by the many ducks that call Aylworth Manor home, alongside the farm's chickens, sheep and horses.

The Hosts
John and Joanna are the most caring hosts you could wish to stay with. Joanna formerly worked in the City before settling at Aylworth whilst John is a dentist. As well as having a busy family life they also run the farm whilst every other spare minute is spent with their horses which they are passionate about.

The Location
Just a short drive from Bourton-on-the-Water. Close to Stow-on-the-Wold, Sudeley Castle, Chedworth Roman Villa, Snowshill Manor, Hidcote Manor, Kiftsgate Court Gardens, amongst other attractions. Close by is Cheltenham with its music, racing and literature festivals whilst beyond is Gloucester with its historic docks and Cathedral.

Rooms (per person per night incl. breakfast)

1 Super King (6') Yellow Room (en suite)	from £55
1 Twin (2 x 3'6") Pink Room (private)	from £50
1 King Size (5') Red Room (private)	from £45
Single Supplement	£15

Meals

Supper	£25
Dinner	£30
(Both by prior arrangement)	

Opening Times
Open all year

Payment Options

Facilities & Services

The Property

A classic Georgian house in Jane Austen country, The Old Rectory is set in an acre of walled garden in the centre of the village, close to National Trust land.   Glimpses of the church next door can be seen from the large terrace, perfect for eating outside. There is a pond and a croquet lawn in the peaceful garden in which there is colour and interest throughout the seasons. There are some specimen trees which are the owners' pride and joy.

The house is traditionally and comfortably furnished and is, above all, a much loved home.

The Hosts

Friendliness and relaxation are the keynotes in Robin and Phyllida's home and they love the diversity of guests. Robin is a retired publisher and Phyllida was, for many years, involved with the Garden Museum (formerly The Museum of Garden History) which was founded by her parents. She organises garden visits in England and abroad and the beautiful garden is a testament to the fact that she is an imaginative gardener whose husband does all the real hard graft!

The Location

It is five miles from Jane Austen's house and museum at Chawton. Portsmouth Dockyard (with HMS Victory, The Mary Rose and Warrior), Gun Wharf Quays and the ferries to the continent and the Isle of Wight are half an hour away. Glorious Goodwood with its racing, classic car events and Festival of Speed is less than 40 minutes drive, as are Winchester and Chichester, with its Cathedral and theatre. Petworth House is closer with its Turners and grounds laid out by Capability Brown. We are convenient for Grange Park Opera and the Watercress Line steam railway runs between Alresford and Alton. Heathrow and Gatwick can be reached within the hour.

Robin and Phyllida Smeeton
The Old Rectory,
Headley, Hampshire GU35 8PW
Tel: 01428 714123
phyllida.smeeton@btinternet.com **1998**

Finding Us

A3 south of Guildford to Hindhead Tunnel. Immediately after tunnel, take first slip road signed Hindhead & Grayshott.
A3 north, take last slip BEFORE the tunnel, signed Hindhead & Grayshott. Go through Grayshott and at Beech Hill garage (approx 4 miles from A3) keep left. Continue to Headley village green, follow road up hill. At top of hill, turn right leaving chestnut tree on island on left and The Hollybush pub on right. House is first drive on left after church.

Rooms (per person per night incl. breakfast)

1 Twin (2 x 3') Room (en suite)	**£50**
1 Twin (2 x 3') Room (private)	**£40**
Single Supplement	**£10**

Meals

Dinner	**£27.50**

Opening Times

Closed Christmas, New Year & Easter

Payment Options

Facilities & Services

The Property

Winchfield House has been the home of Henrietta's family, the Charringtons, for the last five generations. This magnificent Grade II listed Georgian house, built in 1760, was recently renovated by Henrietta and is filled throughout with family antiques and glorious paintings. The bedrooms and bathrooms are spacious and comfortable with imaginative fabrics used to stunning effect.

The house is surrounded by a large garden, swimming pool, parkland and a lake. The Dressage School operates from the 19th century stable block, and dressage classes can often be watched from the arena in the old walled garden.

The Hosts

Henrietta is married to Andrew Wigram. They are both great fun, vivacious and sociable and thoroughly enjoy welcoming guests to their house. Both are energetic organisers and have travelled extensively around Europe and Australasia. Henrietta is on the Board of an American Charity School in Cambodia and they both go and teach there every year. Andrew, who was formerly in the Army and a farmer, runs the estate. Adrian and Ramona, who come from Romania, assist Henrietta and Andrew with the Wolsey Lodge guests and are first class cooks.

The Location

Superbly located in the heart of the countryside near to the M3, there is easy access to London, Heathrow Airport, Windsor and Ascot. London is under one hour by train from Winchfield Station. Other local places of interest are West Green House (garden open and opera season July/August), The Vyne (National Trust), Stratfield Saye and the charming Georgian village of Odiham. Winchester, Salisbury and Portsmouth are all within an hour by car, as are many race courses.

Henrietta & Andrew Wigram
Winchfield House
Odiham Road
Hook
Hampshire RG27 8BS
Tel: 01252 843181 or 07768 730552
henriettawigram@gmail.com   **1983**

Finding Us

From M3 take Junction 5. Take exit to Farnham (A287) over small roundabout and keep on same road. After 1 mile turn left on B3016 signed Hartley Wintney. Continue for 3 miles (do not turn right for station). Pass under M3, entrance is 600 yards on right through white gateway.

Rooms (per person per night incl. breakfast)

2 Double (4'6") Rooms (en suite)		£65
1 Twin (2 x 3') Room (private)		£65
Single Supplement		£20

Meals

Supper	£25
Dinner	£35

(Both by prior arrangement)

Opening Times

Closed Christmas & New Year

Payment Options

Facilities & Services

Amanda Hall & Jon Devereux
Harvest House
Lymington Road, Milford-on-Sea
Lymington, Hampshire SO41 0QN
Tel: 01590 644579 or 07855 443898
amanda@harvesthouse-newforest.co.uk
www.harvesthouse-newforest.co.uk 1970

Finding Us

From Lymington: Continue west on A337.
Approaching Everton bear left signed Milford
on B3058. Harvest House is 1 mile from
turning, on left hand side.
From Highcliffe: East on A337 towards
Lymington. Take 3rd exit off roundabout
marked Milford on B3058. After 3 miles pass
through village with village green on your
right. Harvest House is 500 yards travelling
away from the village on right.

The Property

'A little tranquillity in a busy world' describes the supremely
comfortable Harvest House in Hampshire. Built in the 1920's
as a vicarage, to a design by the well known architect Wm
Ravenscroft and originally boasting a garden designed by
Gertrude Jekyll, it is situated in the quintessentially English
and vibrant village of Milford-on-Sea, in the heart of sailing
country and with beautiful Solent views.

The generous guest sitting room with wood burning
stove, sofas, computer, games and television adjoins the
guest breakfast room, with separate tables, which offers
unobstructed views across the lawns to the Solent and
Isle of Wight beyond. Here guests enjoy the breakfast
of their choice, made to order using local New Forest
Marque produce as availability allows. The wide staggered
staircase leads up to the spacious guest bedrooms and the
attic suite above.

Ample gated off street secure parking is available and storage
for bicycles or cycle hire can be arranged but guests are
welcome to relax and enjoy the immediate surroundings.

The Hosts

Amanda, a retired company director, and her partner Jon
enjoy welcoming guests to Harvest House, Amanda's
family home. Sharing a love of classic cars, they are pleased
to show their collection to any like minded guests. With
their children now grown up, the next generation of little
ones keep them busy. They enjoy walking their two friendly
lurchers in the local Hampshire countryside.

The Location

Milford on Sea, on the coastal boundary of the New Forest,
is a great place to spend a few days. Nearby Lymington is a
'yachties' paradise and Beaulieu, with its famous Abbey and
National Motor Museum is not far. Boat trips, ferries to the
Isle of Wight and National Trust properties are just a short
drive away. Also convenient for the historic naval dockyard
at Portsmouth.

Rooms (per person per night incl. breakfast)

1 King Size (5') Suite (en suite)	**£52.50-£55**
2 Super King (6')/Twin Rooms (en suite)	**£50-£52.50**
Single Supplement	**£20-£30**
Minimum 2 night stay	

Meals
Breakfast only

Opening Times
Open 11 April - 8 November. Open in
December for groups of 4 or more.

Payment Options

Facilities & Services

The Property

This pretty Victorian cottage with its quintessentially English garden, including thriving 'Peter Rabbit' vegetable patch, has climbing roses and wafts of fresh lavender. Its renovation was a labour of love, resulting in a contemporary interior with hints of nostalgia and a fabulous melange of interesting furniture and art.

Guests are welcomed with afternoon tea taken in the gorgeous sitting room or garden, weather permitting. Each cosy bedroom is individually furnished. One is en-suite (with an adjoining single bedroom available – ideal for families) and the other with private bathroom. The standard double beds have sumptuous pillows and fine linens, alongside hospitality trays and other touches. The bathrooms are superb.

Delicious breakfasts, served en famille in the elegant dining room, offer specialities such as porridge, kedgeree or 'Mrs Morgan's Omelettata' to set you up for the day. Evening meals are available for longer staying guests with prior notice and, as with breakfast, ingredients are locally sourced including some from Marne Cottage's own garden.

The Hosts

Cordon Bleu trained cook Julia worked in interior design, evident from her skilful blending of modern and antique furnishings in her fabulous home. Her career has also included teaching and working for Commonwealth organisations and art galleries, as well as professional flower arranging and charity fundraising. The perfect host, with immense local knowledge, Julia will recommend pubs and restaurants, and can even provide picnic hampers.

The Location

This peaceful location offers easy access to Winchester and the Georgian town, Alresford. The New Forest, South Downs National Parks, Jane Austen country, Portsmouth, Southampton and Grange Park Opera are a short drive away and it provides the perfect finale for South Downs walkers. With much to see and do for all age groups and interests, National Trust properties, museums and theatres also abound.

Mrs Julia Morgan
Marne Cottage
Kilmeston Road
Kilmeston
Hampshire SO24 0NJ
Tel: 01962 771418
info@marnecottagebandb.co.uk
www.marnecottagebandb.co.uk   1969

Finding Us

From Winchester (A34/M3 J9), after 5 miles on A272, turn right at Cheriton/Kilmeston crossroads. Immediately after crossroads pass Hopton's Retreat and two houses on left. Marne Cottage's drive is next left; a sign on right telephone post will direct you. Marne Cottage can be found top left hand side of drive.

Rooms (per person per night incl. breakfast)

1 Double (4'6") Room (private)	**£55**
1 Double (4'6") Room (en suite)	**£55**
Single Supplement	**£20**

Meals

Supper (2 Courses)	**£27.50**
Dinner (3 Courses)	**£37.50**

(Both by prior arrangement)

Opening Times

Open all year

Payment Options

Facilities & Services

Peter & Heather Clark
The Noverings
Brook Lane
Bosbury
Ledbury
Herefordshire HR8 1QD
Tel: 01531 641785
info@thenoverings.co.uk
www.thenoverings.co.uk   5943

Finding Us

Detailed directions available on request or at **www.thenoverings.co.uk**

Rooms (per person per night incl. breakfast)

2 Super King (6') Rooms (en suite)	£50-£60
1 Twin (2 x 3') Room (en suite)	£45
Single Supplement	£15-£55

Meals

2 Course supper - by prior arrangement	£20

Opening Times

Open 1 April – 31 October

Payment Options

Facilities & Services

The Property

Between the market town of Ledbury and the Malverns, in the heart of Herefordshire, The Noverings is an Edwardian country house with a most distinctive atmosphere and a real pleasure for guests to enjoy. Surrounded by 17 acres of woodland and large formal garden, with many seating areas, The Noverings has been in the same family for nearly 50 years and has been recently refurbished to offer guests luxurious and spacious accommodation where 'all the little things that matter' have been thoughtfully provided.

The three capacious guests rooms with comfortable seating areas, large en suite bathroom or shower room, are furnished with fresh fabrics and linen and enjoy fine views across the countryside and garden. Downstairs, original oak panelling and decorative features are redolent of the elegance of the Edwardian era and lend the house a warm and relaxing ambience. A sunny terrace can be enjoyed in the summer or relax in the billiard room on cooler days.

Whether it is smoked salmon with scrambled eggs, pancakes or traditional breakfast made from abundant local fare to excellent local restaurants to suit all tastes, your stay here is complete on every front.

The Hosts

Heather and Peter Clark were both solicitors before taking over The Noverings from Heather's parents. Together they have worked to restore the house and gardens and welcome their many guests to enjoy the house they so clearly love. Both are accomplished cooks and as keen walkers, their local knowledge will help you to make the most of your stay.

The Location

Malvern's Three Counties Show Ground famous for Spring and Autumn Garden Shows and the host cities of the Three Choirs Festival Worcester, Hereford and Gloucester are within easy reach as are Eastnor Castle, Hampton Court Castle, the Forest of Dean, and for walkers and cyclists the Herefordshire Trail and Cider Route.

The Property

Brook House is set in a tranquil corner of West Wight, just a 15 minute stroll from the beach, and perfectly situated to explore the whole island. Brook House sits in quiet and mature gardens, with three acres to explore and many lovely spots to sit and enjoy.

In the house, a seamless blend of the original architecture and more recent renovations mark the passage of time from its original Georgian construction and the result is bright, airy and spacious rooms with fine furnishings and décor . In the cooler months, there are wood burning stoves to enjoy.

The three guest rooms are well appointed with care, to ensure guests' comfort. Doubles are king size or larger. The ground floor room has a private shower room whilst on the first floor, one of the two guest rooms has an en suite bathroom and the other an en suite shower room. Island sourced ingredients are a key part of breakfast and supper.

The Hosts

Geoff and Belinda have owned Brook House since 1998, gradually moving here completely from London. Belinda was a solicitor, and Geoff worked in broadcast technology. With his spare time, Geoff enjoys working with a group to build a significant model railway, whilst Belinda works from home, as well as enjoying cooking and gardening.

The Location

The island is full of stunning scenery and history, with over 500 miles of lovely footpaths to enjoy and a wealth of other attractions. From Osborne House and Carisbrooke Castle to the Garlic Farm and the Needles and fossil hunting on the local beach. There are great pubs and restaurants to choose from too.

Geoff & Belinda Walters
Brook House
Brook
Isle of Wight PO30 4EJ
Tel: 01983 740535
bookings@brookhouseiow.co.uk
www.brookhouseiow.co.uk   1971

Finding Us

From B3401 (Newport to Freshwater road) take B3399 at Chessell. After about a mile, pass Brook Church (on left) and on next bend turn right (signed Brook). Then in a few yards, turn right into the gated private road for the Brook House Private Estate. Brook House is in front of you at the bottom of the hill.

Rooms (per person per night incl. breakfast)

2 King Size (5') Rooms (en suite) from **£50**

1 King Size (5') Room (private) from **£55**

Single Supplement   **£20**

Meals

Supper (2 courses)   **£25**
(By prior arrangement)

Opening Times

Closed Christmas & New Year

Payment Options

Facilities & Services

Mrs Raili Fraser
The Old Rectory,
Hallaton, Market Harborough,
Leicestershire LE16 8TY
Tel: 01858 555350
Fax: 01858 555350
oldrectoryhallaton@hotmail.com   **7998**

Finding Us

Take the A47 from Uppingham and turn
left at East Norton and follow signs, or take
A6 from Market Harborough, turn right
onto B6047. After 3 miles turn right. You
will then come to Church Langton and
follow signs to Hallaton.

The Property

A long gravelled drive leads to this Grade II former rectory,
standing proudly on a hill next to the church in this lovely
Leicestershire village in the heart of the rural countryside.
The building has many unique features, and was externally
decorated using crests and stone figurines dating back to 1732.

Guests are greeted warmly and are offered welcoming
afternoon tea served in the drawing room. An imposing oak
staircase leads past guest dining rooms and lounge to a
galleried landing and beautifully decorated king size,
twin and single bedded guest rooms - all with televisions,
hospitality trays and quality toiletries.

The bedrooms overlook the traditional fruit orchard, formal
topiary yew trees, landscaped flower beds and a walnut tree
known to be grown from walnuts taken from a renowned
Motte and Bailey castle mound in Hallaton in the 11th
century.

The Hosts

Raili was a nursing sister and is now dedicated to making
sure guests enjoy all that the family home has to offer, aided
by her daughter, Alexandra, who used to work in finance in
London.

The Location

The heart of England offers a wealth of historic houses and
stately homes to discover. Rutland Water, Britain's largest
man-made lake with bird watching, sailing, windsurfing,
cycling and fly fishing is close by, not to mention
Uppingham, Rockingham Castle, Kelmarsh Hall and many
other houses and lovely gardens to visit are nearby. The
traditional "Bottle Kicking" village festival dating back to
medieval times, takes place in Hallaton on Easter Monday.

Rooms (per person per night incl. breakfast)

1 Single (4'6") Room	(en suite)	**£47.50**
1 Super King (6') Room (en suite)		**£50**
1 Twin (2 x 3') Room	(private)	**£50**
Single Supplement		**£10**

Meals
Breakfast only

Opening Times
Closed Christmas

Payment Options

Facilities & Services

Linda and Tim Jee
Horseshoe Cottage Farm,
Roecliffe Road, Cropston,
Leicestershire LE7 7HQ
Tel: 0116 2350038
lindajee@horseshoecottagefarm.com
www.horseshoecottagefarm.com 7982

Finding Us

From South exit M1 at junction 21A onto the A46, take second exit to Anstey & Beaumont Leys. From North exit M1 at junction 23 onto A512 towards Ashby, at the traffic lights turn left towards Cropston. For more details please see the website above or telephone.

The Property

Luxury in Leicestershire's Charnwood Forest awaits at Horseshoe Cottage Farm, recently converted from old stone farm buildings. It is surrounded by countryside and located in the National Forest, midway between Leicester and Loughborough.

On arrival, guests can enjoy tea and Aga baked scones or homemade cakes, served on the terrace or by the inglenook fireplace in the elegant drawing room. Stone flagged floors and large oak beams in many rooms impart a sense of peacefulness and well-being. Traditional antique furniture graces the interior, especially in the pretty en suite guest bedrooms. Individually decorated with quality fabrics and furnishings, they are a haven of relaxation and the ground floor bedroom is ideal for guests less able to climb stairs.

The cottage garden with herbaceous borders, topiary, azalea and heather beds is home to flourishing kitchen gardens and an orchard where hens lay fresh eggs for breakfast. Fields beyond are laced with footpaths and Bradgate Country Park, with its herds of deer and the ruins of Lady Jane Grey's family home, make a perfect pre-dinner stroll.

The Hosts

Tim, who used to work in the City and Linda, a radiographer and keen gardener, are both well travelled and offer good food, good company and a warm and friendly welcome. Breakfast is a feast and dinner an occasion - clearly Tim and Linda enjoy good food and entertaining!

The Location

Guests are spoilt for choice with so many attractions within an hour: King Richard III Exhibition, Bosworth Battlefield, Stratford-upon-Avon, Warwick and Belvoir Castles, National Space Centre, Stoneywell, Rutland Water, Peak District, NEC and Mallroy & Donnington race track. Just 10 minutes off the M1, 20 minutes from East Midlands airport and mid-way between London and Scotland.

Rooms (per person per night incl. breakfast)

2 King Size (5') Rooms (en suite)	**£50**
1 Super King (6')/Twin Room (en suite)	**£50**
Single Supplement	**£15**

Meals

Supper	**£20**
Dinner	**£30**

Opening Times

Open all year

Payment Options

Facilities & Services

The Property

Glebe House is surrounded by sixteen acres of parkland with views of nearby Belvoir Castle and the pretty church. This gracious listed Georgian home, a former rectory, offers luxury accommodation. Despite the Nottingham address it is firmly located in rural Leicestershire, perfectly placed for guests travelling north or south on the A1 to explore Lincoln, Stamford, Nottingham and unspoilt countryside.

The tree lined driveway leads to a warm welcome from Carole and Andrew with tea and home-made cakes. You will feel instantly 'at home' in the splendidly comfortable Music Room and can unwind and relax in this elegant home. Taking inspiration from the house's Georgian heritage, all the guest rooms are spacious, light and beautifully decorated and furnished in keeping with the period of the house. Fine linen, toiletries, WiFi, and the little touches appreciated by guests, like fresh flowers, are all there for you to enjoy.

Outside, are orchards, a huge vegetable garden, stable yard and paddocks, as well as a formal garden with croquet lawn. Local produce is at the heart of the delicious meals, with fresh homemade bread each morning.

The Hosts

Before retirement Andrew was a Headmaster and Lecturer, but also has been a Civil Servant and Wine Shipper. Carole has a long history in the diplomatic service which saw her travel the world. Together they share a love of choral singing, gardening and of course looking after their guests.

The Location

Glebe House with associations with poets George Crabbe and Lord Byron, is perfectly placed for visiting the Vale of Belvoir, an area of natural beauty on the borders of Leicestershire, Nottinghamshire and Lincolnshire. This unspoilt rural area has wonderful villages, churches and appeals to cyclists and walkers. Burghley House, Belvoir Castle, Newark Antiques Fair, cricket at Trent Bridge and rowing events at Holme Pierrepont draw guests here throughout the year.

Andrew & Carole Brownridge
Glebe House, 26 Church Lane, Muston, Nottingham, Leicestershire NG13 0FD
Tel: 01949 842993 or 07947 742413
glebehouse@glebehousemuston.co.uk
www.glebehousemuston.co.uk   7978

Finding Us

Turn from the A1 onto the A52 near Grantham travel 4 miles towards Nottingham. Close to the sign for Leicestershire border turn left at The Gap Inn (signed to Muston). Glebe House is 300 yards on the left hand side of the road. Hosts will collect guests from Grantham or Bottesford train stations.

Rooms   (per person per night incl. breakfast)

1 King Size (5') Four Poster Room (en suite)	**£60-£95**
1 King Size (5') Room (en suite)	**£55-£80**
1 Double (4'6") Four Poster or Twin (2 x 3') Room (private)	**£45-£80**
One night supplement	**£5**
Single Supplement	**£15**
Discounts available for 2 nights or more	

Meals

Supper (2 courses)	**£20**
Dinner (4 courses)	**£30**
(Both occasionally by prior arrangement)	

Opening Times

Closed occasionally

Payment Options

Facilities & Services

Mrs Nicki Dalton
Hrempis Farm
58 Main Street, Rempstone, Loughborough
Leicestershire LE12 6RH
Tel: 01509 881285 or 07725 429749
bookings@hrempisfarm.co.uk
www.hrempisfarm.co.uk　　　　7977

The Property

Hrempis Farm is an 18th century, Grade II listed farmhouse on the Leicestershire/Nottinghamshire border in the heart of the Quorn Hunt country. It enjoys a degree of solitude being set amidst its own grounds and is close to the village centre.

Your arrival is marked with a welcoming tea, served before open fires in the drawing room, in the warm sunlit conservatory or enjoy the summerhouse overlooking the gardens and paddock. An abundance of fine art and local pottery adorn the house along with a plentiful supply of books, whilst a full size snooker table, a grand piano and, in the summer, croquet on the lawns can all be enjoyed.

One guest room on the first floor has a four poster bed, whilst the other, with a twin/double bed is on the second floor, both with views across the gardens. With private sitting rooms and bathrooms, each has been furnished with luxury in mind. If travelling on business, Hrempis Farm provides free WiFi and a desk in each suite.

Breakfast and supper feature local and fair-trade produce. Formal dinners can also be arranged on request. There are excellent local pubs and restaurants all within easy reach including the 2 Michelin star Restaurant Sat Bains.

The Hosts

Before bringing up a family Nicki was a journalist and now has her own PR company as well as being a local school governor, parish councillor, National Trust volunteer at nearby Calke Abbey and area president of Save the Children.

The Location

Hrempis Farm is a 'foodies' heaven with the world famous Stilton cheese and Melton Mowbray pork pies made close by. Robin Hood country and the Peak District National Park are within reach and Burghley Horse Trials, Quorn Hunt Meet, Newark International Antiques Fair, racing at Donnington and Mallory Park, cricket at Trent Bridge, rugby, horseracing, theatre and food fairs can all be enjoyed.

Finding Us

Exit M1J24. Follow A6 towards Hathern, turn left onto A6006. Follow for 5 miles until to traffic lights, straight into Rempstone village. Follow road around bend, Hrempis Farm is on right, facing the turning signed for Wysall. From Loughborough, take A60 towards Nottingham to traffic lights at Rempstone village. Turn right into village, follow road around the bend and Hrempis Farm is on right.

Rooms (per person per night incl. breakfast)

1 Super King (6')/Twin Room (en suite)	**£55-£70**
1 King Size (5') Four Poster Room (private)	**£55-£70**
1 Double (4'6") Room (private)	**£55**
Single Supplement	**£20**

Meals

Supper (3 courses) (By prior arrangement)	**£25**

Opening Times
Closed Christmas

Payment Options

Facilities & Services

The Property

A listed Georgian manor house, lovingly restored by its present owners and nestling in secluded gardens in the village centre.

Guests are welcomed with refreshments on arrival, usually served in the spacious kitchen. On the first floor there are two light and capacious guest rooms, both en suite, one a bathroom (complete with roll top bath) and the other a deluxe shower room. On the second floor, a further large king size room, a small single (occasional double) and a twin bedded room are all en suite. Rooms are individually decorated, luxuriously furnished and are very well appointed.

In fine weather guests can enjoy the garden, which includes a croquet lawn. Bicycles are available for exploring further afield. With Cordon Bleu standard evening meals and breakfasts including homemade granola, jams and marmalade with local eggs, bacon and sausages, Breedon Hall is justifiably proud of its culinary reputation.

The Hosts

Charlotte, a mother to two young sons is a professional caterer and runs all manner of events at the Hall. She grew up in the area and husband Charles, a business consultant, is also a local district councillor. Both love entertaining and are a mine of information on local places to visit. There are two outstanding pubs, one gastro, the other traditional, within walking distance.

The Location

On the Leicestershire/Derbyshire border this is an ideal location for a stopover as it is just off the M1. Located within the National Forest, Breedon is in fact in Leicestershire, but the postal address is Derbyshire and it borders Nottinghamshire and Staffordshire! East Midlands Airport is only 5 minutes away by car. It is close to several National Trust properties and Donington Park race track. Numerous cultural activities are available throughout the year for music lovers, horticulturists and foodies in Melbourne and Ashby de la Zouch is a popular market town with regular farmers' markets.

Charles & Charlotte Meynell
Breedon Hall, Breedon-on-the-Hill
Leicestershire DE73 8AN
Tel: 01332 864935 or 07973 105467
enquiries@breedonhall.co.uk
www.breedonhall.co.uk　　　　7972

Finding Us

From M1, take J24A towards East Midlands Airport. Bypass airport continue on A453 into Breedon-on-the-Hill village. Breedon Hall is opposite the Three Horseshoes. From A42, take off-ramp at J13 for Ashby de la Zouch. Left towards Ashby then right at roundabout on B587 (Nottingham Road) towards Breedon. Drive into village and Three Horseshoes on right just after turning to Worthington. Hall immediately on left.

Rooms　(per person per night incl. breakfast)

2 Super King (6') Rooms (en suite)		£65
1 Super King (6') Room (en suite)		£55
1 Twin Room (2 x 3') (en suite)		£47.50
1 Single (4'6") Room (en suite)		£75

Meals

Dinner	£35
(3 courses inc.1 bottle of wine)	
Kitchen Supper	£25
(2 courses inc.1 bottle of wine)	

Opening Times

Closed Christmas & occasionally

Payment Options

Facilities & Services

The Property

This 1720 Georgian farm house enjoys a spectacular hilltop position with outstanding views across the Lincolnshire countryside.

Elegantly and sympathetically restored in 2002 Brills Farm House is the family home for this working arable and livestock farm. Filled with original features, antique furniture, huge fireplaces and beautiful materials, guests are able to enjoy the amazing views from the stylish rooms and large comfortable beds. Bathrooms, while period in decor, have all modern amenities with deep baths, power showers and lots of hot water!

Extensive woodland and a beautiful lake can be explored by walkers and animal lovers alike. With aspects to enjoy in all seasons this is truly a place to stay at any time of year.

The Hosts

You are welcomed to Brills Farm by Charlie and Sophie White and their growing family of four children. Well versed in the art of comfort, the children help Sophie to ensure that relaxation and enjoyment feature top of your stay. Sophie, as a well travelled and experienced Chef will provide you with sumptuous breakfasts and delectable evening meals sourced from Charlie's 2000 acre farm, the house garden and local suppliers.

The Location

With National Trust gems in every direction and awe inspiring Lincoln with its stunning Cathedral & Castle an easy 15 minutes drive away, this is a great location from which to explore. Newark International Antiques fair and river boat cruises, boutique shopping and Eden Hall Spa on the doorstep. Water skiing, Belton International Horse trials and evening racing at Southwell Racecourse may tempt those of the sportier nature.

Charlie & Sophie White
Brills Farm,
Brills Hill, Norton Disney, Lincoln,
Lincolnshire LN6 9JN
Tel: 01636 892311 or 07947 136228
admin@brillsfarm-bedandbreakfast.co.uk
www.brillsfarm-bedandbreakfast.co.uk 7985

Finding Us

From the A1, take A46 direction Lincoln. At roundabout follow A46. Take the first exit for Norton Disney. At T-junction turn right and follow for ½ mile. Take first left turn, follow for 1 mile and the drive entrance is on right before going up the hill.

Rooms (per person per night incl. breakfast)

1 Super King (6') Room (en suite)	£48
1 Super King (6')/Twin Room (en suite)	£48
1 Double (4'6") Room (en suite)	£48
Single Occupancy	£58

Meals

Supper	£20
Dinner	£30

(By arrangement – minimum 6 guests)

Opening Times

Closed Christmas & New Year

Payment Options

Facilities & Services

Jane and Simon Wright
The Barn,
Spring Lane, Folkingham,
Lincolnshire NG34 0SJ
Tel: 01529 497199 or 07876 363292
Fax: 01529 497199
sjwright@farming.co.uk
www.thebarnspringlane.co.uk   7983

Finding Us

From the A15 in Folkingham, turn into Spring Lane alongside the Village Hall, (just below the old school and the Market Place). The Barn is a little way along on the right.

The Property

The Barn, Grade II listed, is tucked away in eight acres of grassland on the edge of the lovely conservation village of Folkingham. During its conversion, the owners discovered ancient stonework, apparently already 'recycled' in the 17th century from the nearby Norman castle.

Restored with minimum interference to the original building, open beamed areas were retained and under floor heating installed. Open log fires, comfortable sofas, antique oak furniture and a large dining table now reside where grain was once thrashed. French windows from the kitchen, formerly stables, lead to the courtyard garden. Guests enjoy pretty bed linens, in simply styled rooms, with excellent power showers and lovely views.

The Hosts

Simon and Jane farmed nearby until they discovered The Barn. Still producing much of their own delicious food, including Lincolnshire sausages, they keep rare breed chickens and sheep, and, in the season, enjoy fish and game from Simon's days out. Great hosts, they love entertaining and always eat with guests wanting an evening meal. Simon also enjoys flying an ancient aeroplane, and Jane takes to her bicycle, when she has time.

The Location

Folkingham has been described as a 'Georgian rural gem'. The village centre has changed very little, the village stores, and the Greyhound, a former coaching Inn, still stand in the Market Place, near the church, dating from the 12th century. There are several good eating establishments nearby. South Lincolnshire comes as a surprise to those who think the county is only flat, the villages are surrounded by gently rolling land and linked by generally deserted lanes. All perfect for cycling or walking. Numerous country houses such as Burghley and Belton, outstanding churches and cathedrals, and busy market towns, are all within easy reach and Stamford is always a favourite.

Rooms   (per person per night incl. breakfast)

1 Super King (6')/Twin Room (en suite)	**£40-£45**
1 Double (4' 6") Room (en suite)	**£40-£45**
1 Single (3') Room (private)	**£55**
Single Supplement	**£20**

Meals

Supper	**£17.50**
Dinner	**£25**

Opening Times

Closed Christmas & New Year

Payment Options

Facilities & Services

The Property
This classic Regency townhouse is located in one of the most beautiful and sought-after terraces in Stamford. Built in 1830 in the local honey-coloured limestone, with views across the meadows to the valley beyond, it is just a short walk to the cobbled streets of this elegant town that has been preserved in time by its conservation status. Popular with tourists and movie directors, it was the setting chosen for the BBC's Middlemarch.

Guests enjoy tea on arrival in the lovely drawing room or in the tranquil walled rear garden. There is a choice of two peaceful and elegant double bedrooms with private bath/ shower rooms, decorated in restful colours with Designer's Guild bed linen.

Breakfast, using the finest local ingredients, sets visitors up for the day and is enjoyed in the dining room overlooking the Welland Vale.

The Hosts
Christine and Robert having so enjoyed indulgent hospitality when staying at Wolsey Lodges decided to become hosts themselves and want others to fall under the spell of their lovely home of 20 years. Christine cooks delicious suppers by prior arrangement and is also pleased to recommend the many fabulous local pubs and restaurants and share their detailed local knowledge for walks and sightseeing.

The Location
While handy for the A1 Great North Road Stamford's central location also places it at the point where five counties meet (Leicestershire, Northamptonshire, Cambridgeshire, Lincolnshire and Rutland). So there's always plenty to do whatever your interests. Its proximity to numerous National Trust and other historic houses as well as nearby towns such as Ely, Newark, Melton Mowbray and Cambridge (only an hour away), make Stamford a popular weekend destination. The house is only a 15 minute walk from the local railway station.

Robert & Christine Caldecott
12 Rutland Terrace
Stamford
Lincolnshire PE9 2QD
Tel: 07957 828931
robert.caldecott@virgin.net   **7973**

Finding Us
Northbound or Southbound on A1 - Take B6121 in to Stamford. After about ½ mile, cross mini roundabout. No 12 is on your left. By rail Stamford has its own railway station which is about 15 minutes walk from the house. It is well connected cross country to Birmingham (westbound) and Peterborough, Cambridge and Stansted (eastbound). Peterborough is on the King's Cross mainline.

Rooms (per person per night incl. breakfast)

2 Double (4'6") Rooms (private)	**£45**
Single Supplement	**£15**

Meals

Supper (2 Courses)	**£20**
(By prior arrangement)	

Opening Times
Closed Christmas

Payment Options

Facilities & Services

The Property

This distinguished house in SE14, sits above a carpet of twinkling London lights overlooking the landscaped Telegraph Hill Park.

The cosy, yet spacious, reception rooms are truly welcoming and have a quiet air of elegance which flows through to beautifully decorated and furnished bedrooms and sparkling bathrooms. The Chinese Peony Room has the plushest of carpets, the biggest of beds, the crispest of linens, Chinese porcelain lamps, lacquered panels and kimonos in the wardrobe. Upstairs, the Tulip Room is decorated with tulip and flower prints. The Richmond Room has twin beds, an adjacent private bathroom, and enjoys a view of the garden.

The exquisite garden was laid out by David's late father, Tim who was a great gardener. It is a perfect lure for garden lovers. There are vibrant camellias, two majestic, fully grown magnolias, a catalpa, holly and bay trees.

Wolsey Lodge guests looking for luxury in London need look no further - you've arrived!

The Host

David Marten and his family have taken over the B&B from David's late mother, Anne. David and Maedhbhina are warm hosts who like to provide the best hospitality for their guests. In addition to bed and breakfast they also run a photography school. They are passionate about food and travel and like nothing more than to go for a good walk with their dogs.

The Location

113 Pepys Road is lucky to have unrestricted parking to make it easy to come and go as you wish, although the nearest mainline and underground station, New Cross Gate, will get you to London Bridge in just 5 minutes and to Westminster in 20. Greenwich, The Cutty Sark, The National Maritime Museum, Dulwich Picture Gallery, Horniman Museum and Tate Modern are places of interest nearby. The City Airport is only half an hour away by car.

David Marten
113 Pepys Road
London SE14 5SE
Tel: 020 7639 1060
davidmarten@pepysroad.com
www.pepysroad.com 4696

Finding Us

From Elephant & Castle roundabout, take A2 (New Kent Road, Old Kent Road, New Cross Road), proceed till turning to Sainsburys Supermarket. Turn left into this turn, then turn right to get back to New Cross Road. After short distance, turn left into Pepys Road, go up the hill, No. 113 is opposite Telegraph Hill Park.

Rooms (per person per night incl. breakfast)

1 Super King (6') Room (en suite)	£55
1 Super King (6')/Twin Room (en suite)	£55
1 Super King (6')/Twin Room (private)	£55
Single Supplement	£30

Meals
Breakfast only

Opening Times
Open all year

Payment Options

Facilities & Services

The Property
Tucked away in the heart of Wimbledon village is an exquisite Edwardian house, home to Ronnie and Sue Dunbar and affable Labrador, Wallace. This large house is split into four apartments and Flat 1A spreads out across the ground floor and overlooks the garden. The All England Lawn Tennis Club is on the doorstep, Wimbledon Common is just a short stroll away and you are rarely more than a few minutes from designer shops and cafes aplenty.

Ronnie and Sue are Scottish and together run an interior design business which is evident throughout the house where carefully selected furnishings are interspersed with antiques and modern conveniences like the walk-in shower in the en suite bathroom. The Aga is the central point of the kitchen and meals are enjoyed around the table.

The guest bedroom is well equipped for a comfortable stay and the adjoining sitting room is yours to use exclusively – a great retreat after a day's sightseeing. There is also a small single bedroom available if travelling with a child aged 10 or over. Tea and cake on arrival, delicious breakfasts and dinner if pre-arranged go hand in hand with conversation and laughter to make this Wolsey Lodge a real gem.

The Hosts
Ronnie is a chartered accountant with a keen interest in golf and most other sports and Sue was a nurse before turning her skilled hand to interior design and her other interest is evident in the gorgeous garden here.

The Location
This is such a convenient location - everything is so readily to hand either walking distance, tube or taxi. Shops, tourist attractions and memorable sights can be combined with the enjoyment of London's parks, the closest of which is the 1000 acre Wimbledon Common.

Ronnie & Sue Dunbar
Flat 1A, Alvington House
42 Marryat Road
Wimbledon
London SW19 5BD
Tel: 0208 9468184
sueandronnie2005@yahoo.co.uk   **4693**

Finding Us
By train from Waterloo to Wimbledon. By tube: District line to Wimbledon. Detailed instructions available on request.

Rooms (per person per night incl. breakfast)

1 Twin (2 x 3') Room (en suite)	**£50**
Single occupancy	**£60**

Meals

Supper	**£20**
Dinner	**£28**

Opening Times
Closed Christmas, New Year & Wimbledon fortnight.

Payment Options

Facilities & Services

Sally Anne Chilton
Parklands
10 Parklands Road, London SW16 6TD
Tel: 020 8696 0089 or 07985 219829
info@chilton-hospitality.co.uk
www.parklandsbandb.com   **4691**

Finding Us
Tooting Bec Underground Station 1 mile.
Mainline Railway Balham is 2.4 miles. By
car: A3 M4 and M25 closest Motorways.
Off A214, turning right at traffic lights on
to Church Lane. First left at roundabout on
to Furzedown Drive - straight over mini
roundabout and then first right and first right.
Parklands is fifth house on right.

The Property
Ideally situated for visiting south west London, this lovely
terraced Edwardian house on a quiet, leafy street in
Furzedown, Tooting, has been tastefully restored retaining
key original features but now providing contemporary
luxury, style and masses of charm. It offers easy access to
public transport into town, and on street parking available.
Guests will enjoy the lovely garden when weather permits.

The house is a veritable art gallery, with the owner's love of
contemporary and classic art very much in evidence. The
bedrooms are light and airy, decorated in muted, restful
colours, two double rooms with en suite bathrooms (with
excellent power showers) and one twin with a private
bathroom. Every luxury is provided for guests including an
informative monthly newsletter for guests - with restaurant
recommendations and detailing interesting exhibitions and
shows. Breakfasts, served in the state of the art kitchen,
which opens onto the garden, are exceptional. Sally's
continental breakfasts are renowned and include speciality
breads, homemade cakes, pancakes, scones as well as
preserves.

The Hosts
Sally is a Cordon Bleu cook who worked in hospitality for
many years, as a private chef and latterly running a City
wine bar. She and her sons have enjoyed sharing their
home with guests for over ten years now and the high
number of return visitors is a testament to her skills. Evening
meals are available by prior arrangement.

The Location
This part of London is a perfect base for sports fans visiting
Wimbledon, horticulturists attending RHS flower shows
including Hampton Court or visiting Kew Gardens. Lots of
fabulous restaurants are within a three mile radius and, of
course, all that London has to offer is within half an hour's
journey on public transport.

Rooms (per person per night incl. breakfast)

2 King Size (5') Rooms (en suite)	**£47.50-£52.50**
1 Super King (6')/Twin Room (private)	**£47.50**
Single Supplement	**£27.50**
2 night minimum stay at weekends.	

Meals

Supper (1 course)	**£15**
Dinner (2 courses)	**£25**
(Both by prior arrangement)	

Opening Times
Open all year

Payment Options

Facilities & Services

The Property

The Bassetts will greet you with a warm Anglo-American welcome, ably assisted by Bonnie the Dog, as you arrive at this beautifully restored Grade II listed thatched Norfolk farmhouse. The interior is light, the inglenook fireplace offers the opportunity for warm fires on cold winter evenings, and the conservatory offers a place to enjoy the gardens and birds in all seasons while eating breakfast, sipping tea or enjoying pre-dinner drinks. It is a well-loved home, a perfect place to share warm hospitality, friendship and good food.

The three en suite bedrooms on the first floor (Rossini, Vivaldi and Verdi) are named for composers as befits the home of two musicians. All have fine views of the old flint St Nicholas Church. Both the Bassetts are avid cooks who especially enjoy dining with their guests by candlelight, and sharing with them inventive food using the best of the local ingredients available. The food and décor of the house are both enhanced by their travel experiences in many lands.

The garden at Church Farm House is just under an acre, with two ponds to enhance its charm. Richard prides himself on the changing seasonal displays that the garden offers. Especially colourful are the many varieties of spring tulips, the brilliant summer begonias, late summer dahlias and the hanging baskets filled with winter pansies. The patio, gazebo, swing and hammock all offer comfortable outdoor seating.

The Hosts

Richard and Georgia Bassett originally came to England to teach music. After their international teaching career, they moved to North Lopham where they enjoy sharing life in the countryside with their guests. Church Farm House is also the headquarters for The Association for Music in International Schools, an international music charity which they founded.

The Location

Church Farm House is well situated for visits to Norwich, Bury St. Edmunds, the Suffolk heritage coast, the North Norfolk coast, the Broads and a host of National Trust houses and gardens.

Richard and Georgia Bassett
Church Farm House,
Church Road, North Lopham,
Diss, Norfolk IP22 2LP
Tel: 01379 687270 or 07920 488201
cfhhosts@gmail.com
www.churchfarmhouse.org   3994

Finding Us

Take the A11 to Thetford then A1066 towards Diss. At South Lopham turn to North Lopham in front of White Horse Pub. Continue about 1 mile. Church Farm House is opposite North Lopham church.

Rooms (per person per night incl. breakfast)

1 Single (4') Vivaldi Room (en suite)	**£55**
1 King Size (5') Four Poster Rossini Room (en suite)	**£55**
1 Twin (2 x 3') Verdi Room (en suite)	**£55**
Single Supplement (For double/twin rooms)	**£20**

Meals

Dinner	**£30**

Opening Times

Closed January

Payment Options

Facilities & Services

David & Andra Papworth
Tuttington Hall
Tuttington, Norwich
Norfolk NR11 6TL
Tel: 01263 733417
david@tuttingtonhall.co.uk
www.tuttingtonhall.co.uk   3977

Finding Us

From Norwich head north on A140, on
approach to Aylsham, at roundabout take
3rd exit, signed Cromer. Then take 3rd
right signed Tuttington; through village, at
T-junction turn right, pass church on left,
300m turn right into long gravel drive.

Rooms (per person per night incl. breakfast)

1 Super King (6') Room	(en suite)	**£62.50**
1 King Size (5') Room	(en suite)	**£52.50**
1 Single (3') Room	(en suite)	**£52.50**
Single Supplement		**£15**

Meals

Dinner   **£35**
(By prior arrangement, minimum 4 persons)

Opening Times

Closed Occasionally

Payment Options

Facilities & Services

The Property

Tuttington Hall is a rather special, Grade II listed 18th
century house surrounded by beautifully maintained
gardens and beyond these the farmland that your host
David's family have farmed for some 80 years.

Together David and Andra have managed to create a
wonderful haven of peace and tranquillity for their guests.
On arrival, home baked scones, cakes and tea are served in
the spacious drawing room which is comfortably furnished
with old family pieces and where a welcoming fire awaits
in the colder months. A candlelit dining room or informal
garden room provide the perfect backdrop to the delicious
meals provided which feature home produced meat and
champion sausages. Eggs, bread, fruit, and vegetables are all
either home produced or sourced locally. Fish and shellfish
from the coast, with Cromer crabs a local favourite.

The bedrooms, which include a family friendly suite, each
have a spacious en suite bathroom and are delightfully
decorated and furnished, with fine linen and towels. And
each room offers views across the gardens and surrounding
countryside.

The Hosts

Andra and David lead very busy lives but despite this they
are the most hospitable hosts who go out of their way
to ensure that their guests' needs are met. They are both
enthusiastic cooks and are justifiably proud of the home
produced meat and vegetables they serve.

The Location

Tuttington Hall is within easy reach of both the North
Norfolk coast with its wide sandy beaches and the stunning
Norfolk Broads. There are both links and inland golf courses
only a short drive away. There are a number of historic
houses and gardens including Blickling Hall, along with
the attractive market towns of Holt and Aylsham. The 'Fine
City of Norwich' with its' magnificent Cathedral and Castle
combine to make this a fascinating destination.

The Property

In search of peace and quiet? Then consider the perfect retreat at Manor House Farm. Standing alongside the village church the farm has been home to Libby and Robin for over 40 years and in this time they have transformed it into a beautiful country house with a garden that visitors flock to. Tea and homemade cakes or cookies will mark your arrival.

The converted stable wing, with central heating, is across the courtyard and has two large, airy bedrooms with en suites, a spacious sitting room with wood burning stove and a small kitchen. The twin room has wheelchair access. In the main house there is a double bedroom with en suite bathroom. Furnished to ensure guests' absolute comfort, it is easy to understand why guests return to Manor House Farm time and again.

The four acres of gardens include a striking avenue of pleached limes, an abundance of roses, a sunken courtyard garden and an ornamental greenhouse. Breakfast is served in the dining room overlooking the lawn and home-reared pork, garden fruit and eggs from the family hens are offered and cooked to perfection. A good selection of local restaurants and pubs offer evening meals and Libby and Robin are more than happy to make recommendations. Guests' horses can be stabled here by arrangement.

The Hosts

Robin and Libby have farmed here since 1966, bringing up their four children in what is very much a comfortable family home. Robin is a conservationist and they both have a huge interest in the garden, as well as being widely travelled.

The Location

Once part of the Holkham estate, Manor House Farm is perfectly located to explore the North Norfolk coast, marshes and beaches, Houghton Hall, Sandringham, Blicking, Felbrigg, Oxburgh and Holkham Hall itself as well as Burnham Market, Norwich and Holt and the seal trips from Blakeney are not to be missed.

Robin & Elisabeth Ellis
Manor House Farm
Wellingham
King's Lynn
Norfolk
PE32 2TH
Tel: 01328 838227
Fax: 01328 838348
libby.ellis@btconnect.com
www.manor-house-farm.co.uk　3962

Finding Us

Wellingham is 7 miles from Fakenham and 9 miles from Swaffham, ½ mile off the A1065 north of Weasenham. Manor House Farm is beside the church in Wellingham.

Rooms　(per person per night incl. breakfast)

2 King Size (5') Rooms (en suite)	**£55-£65**
1 Twin (2 x 3') Room (en suite)	**£55-£65**
Single Occupancy	**£65-£75**

Meals

Breakfast only

Opening Times

Open all year

Payment Options

Facilities & Services

The Property

Set amidst a working farm in a conservation area, Castle Farm dates back over 350 years, with later extensions by famous Norfolk architect Thomas Jeckel. The eco-friendly farmhouse is set in beautiful Arts & Crafts landscaped gardens with river access and planned walks to enjoy. Inside, the house is traditionally furnished with antiques and heirlooms from the Carrick family, farmers here since the 1920s.

There is an open fire for colder days and terrace with river views to enjoy tea or just relax while appreciating summer and autumn sunsets. The bedrooms are airy and lavishly furnished with antiques and all manner of luxuries including fine linens, toiletries, bathrobes, tea/coffee facilities and televisions plus ample heat and hot water from the sustainable fuel source. This place is serenely quiet (excepting the occasional goose, owl or fox!).

Delicious breakfasts served en famille and using home-produced ingredients and preserves are relaxed and set guests up for the day. By special arrangement equally good evening meals are available too.

The Hosts

John and Jean are passionate about the environment and sustainability and they farm rare breed animals and poultry under Higher Level Stewardship. A warm welcome, fabulous food, first-hand insight into this stunningly beautiful area, plus recommendations for places and local hostelries to visit (including their own) are just a few of the reasons why guests return time and again to this luxury eco-friendly farmhouse.

The Location

This is a beautiful part of Norfolk. Dereham and Norwich are nearby and the Broads and the North Norfolk Coast less than an hour. Sporting enthusiasts can enjoy walking, cycling, canoeing, fishing and it's perfect for bird watching or painting. With numerous gardens and National Trust properties, museums, steam railways, abbeys and cathedrals to explore, there's something here for all the family to enjoy.

John & Jean Carrick
Carricks at Castle Farm
Elsing Road, Swanton Morley,
Dereham, Norfolk NR20 4JT
Tel: 01362 638302
jean@castlefarm-swanton.co.uk
www.carricksatcastlefarm.co.uk   3958

Finding Us

Take B1147 from A47 at Swanton Morley turn. Follow B1147 through Swanton Morley until Darby's pub, turn right in front of pub and ½ mile up lane on left is drive for Castle Farm. Farmhouse is at the bottom of the drive.

Rooms (per person per night incl. breakfast)

1 Super King (6')/Twin Room (private)	£50
1 Double (4'6") Room (private)	£50
2 Double (4'6") Rooms (en suite)	£50
1 Family Room with Double (4'6") & 1 Twin (2 x 3') (en suite)	£50

Meals

Supper (2 courses)	£20
Dinner (3 courses)	£30

Opening Times

Open all year

Payment Options

Facilities & Services

Liz Jarrett
Colledges House, Oakham Lane,
Staverton, Nr. Daventry,
Northamptonshire NN11 6JQ
Tel: 01327 702737 or 07710 794112
lizjarrett@colledgeshouse.co.uk
www.colledgeshouse.co.uk 4999

The Property

A wonderful welcome awaits in this beautiful Grade II listed, large thatched Northamptonshire stone cottage, with converted barn, conservatory and secluded garden.

There's something special at every turn. Winter evenings are spent in front of a roaring fire in the stunning drawing room. For summer serenity, enjoy the cottage sitting room with its Bechstein piano, or wander into the conservatory to sit and read, away from it all.

Bedrooms in both the main house and cottage are uniquely and individually decorated - a Jacobean trunk in the single, Gothic headboards in the twin - a beautiful bureau in the bathroom. Beds are hugely comfortable and bathrooms include both bath and shower.

The beautiful garden creates surprises in formal and informally designed 'rooms', with harmony and colour contrasts in the inspired planting. Sit on the terrace and watch koi carp swimming in the pond - or relax, listening to the waterfall.

The Hosts

Liz is a warm and gregarious hostess and attended the Cordon Bleu. Her superb meals are legendary with a dinner party atmosphere, mixing great food, company and conversation. By prior arrangement, friends or clients may also be invited.

The Location

The picturesque conservation village of Staverton has magnificent views over open country. It lies on the Jurassic Way and The Three River circular walk passes through the parish. Warwick Castle, Althorp, Woburn and Stratford, are all within easy reach. Colledges House is within 10 - 20 minutes of the M1, M6 and M40, so is ideally located for holiday and weekend breaks, for business or travelling, north or south.

Finding Us

Take the A425. From Daventry, turn right 100 yards after Staverton Park Conference Centre and Golf Course into the village, then first right, keep left, at give way sign turn sharp left and Colledges House is immediately on the right. From Leamington, turn left at The Countryman pub, keep right, at the Green keep straight on into Oakham Lane and Colledges House is the last house on the left.

Rooms (per person per night incl. breakfast)

1 Single (3'6") Room	(en suite)	**£69.50**
2 King Size (5') Rooms	(en suite)	**£49.50**
1 Twin (2 x 3') Room	(en suite)	**£49.50**
Single Supplement		**£20**

Meals

Dinner	**£35**

Opening Times

Open all year

Payment Options

Facilities & Services

George & Deborah Philipson
Preston House
Chathill, Alnwick
Northumberland NE67 5DH
Tel: 01665 589461 or 07817 175609
Fax: 01665 589461
info@northumbrian-escapes.co.uk　　**8948**
www.prestonhousebedandbreakfast.co.uk

Finding Us

Off A1 signed Ellingham, Doxford and Preston and brown tourist sign for Preston Tower (which is opposite the house). Stay on this minor road, pass signs for Ellingham on left, pass school on left and pass Joiners Bunkhouse on left. Preston House is next on left with stone pillared gateway, swing wide to pass through gate, park at front door.

The Property

As perfect a Northumbrian country farmhouse as you could wish to find. Welcoming open fires in winter, comfortable furnishings for relaxation and gardens with fine views over stunning countryside. Built in the early 1800's, Preston House is in the hamlet of Preston, close to Alnwick and home to George and Deborah Philipson since 2009. Newly refurbished, Preston House offers all the modern comforts you could wish for and yet still retains many of the fine features of the original house complemented by antiques sitting gracefully alongside more contemporary furniture and décor.

Each guest room has been lavishly furnished with everything a guest could need for a comfortable night's sleep whilst the en suite shower and bathrooms offer luxury toiletries aplenty. Once rested then breakfast here provides a memorable start to the day with a tempting choice of fayre including Craster kippers, scrambled egg and smoked salmon, fresh fruit and a delicious range of preserves.

The gardens, fortunate to be visited by red squirrels, offer the chance to try a little croquet or just to sit a while and enjoy the simple splendour of a corner of Northumberland.

The Hosts

Up until November 2009 George and Deborah and their family had been farming for generations. A change of lifestyle brought them to Preston House and now its restoration is complete Deborah finds the time to paint whilst George enjoys the challenges of refurbishing old Northumbrian properties.

The Location

Preston House is perfectly located mid-point between Newcastle-upon-Tyne and Edinburgh. Northumberland offers something for everyone – sandy beaches, miles of Hadrian's wall to explore, Bamburgh, Alnwick, Warkworth and Dunstanburgh castles. Farne, Coquet and Holy Islands, Cragside, Wallington and Paxton Houses and gardens.

Rooms　(per person per night incl. breakfast)

4 Super King (6')/Twin Rooms (en suite)	**£60**
Single Occupancy	**£85**

Meals

Breakfast only

Opening Times

Closed Christmas & New Year

Payment Options

Facilities & Services

The Property

Situated in the heart of Northumberland National Park and with views across to the lovely market town of Hexham, Loughbrow House dates from 1780 and is now a family home. It is set in nine acres of beautiful gardens which are open to the public under The National Gardens Scheme. So if you are looking for English country house charm in a nutshell, this is perfect.

Classically furnished with a charming mix of Georgian and Victorian antiques, plus other interesting 'objets' and fine art, the grand drawing room transports guests into a bygone era. There are four spacious guest bedrooms furnished with antiques, all with generously proportioned en suite or private facilities.

Tasty and lovingly prepared full English breakfast is served in the elegant Georgian dining room and includes homemade bread and preserves and delicious fresh coffee.

The Host

Mrs Clark has been welcoming guests for many years and is well known in the area and involved in many charities. As a Cordon Bleu trained cook, Mrs Clark has imparted her secrets to her housekeeper who enjoys preparing dinner (by arrangement) for guests. Mrs Clark makes use of her extensive kitchen garden to provide home produced fruit and vegetables. The family has farmed locally for decades and your host is always pleased to share her detailed local knowledge with you.

The Location

Within easy reach of the A69 Loughbrow House provides a great stopover. Situated 600ft above the River Tyne, looking over the market town of Hexham and onward to the North Tyne Valley.

Mrs Kenneth Clark
Loughbrow House
Hexham
Northumberland
NE46 1RS
Tel: 01434 603351
patriciaclark351@btinternet.com   **8943**
www.loughbrowhousebandb.co.uk

Finding Us
Detailed directions available on request.

Rooms
(per person per night incl. breakfast)

1 King Size (5') Room	(en suite)	**£55-£75**
1 Twin (2 x 3') Room	(en suite)	**£50-£70**
1 Twin (2 x 3') Room	(private)	**£45-£60**
1 Single (1 x 3') Room	(private)	**£40-£60**
Single occupancy of twin or double		**£80-£100**

Meals
Dinner   (3 courses)   **£25**
(By prior arrangement, not on Sunday or Monday)

Opening Times
Closed 22nd December to 3rd January.

Payment Options

Facilities & Services

The Property

Rectory Farm, a beautifully secluded, two hundred and seventy year old, creeper clad Cotswold country house revealed at the end of a tree lined avenue, is situated in its own 450 acre valley of scenic farmland.

Off the traditional flagstoned hall, there is a welcoming drawing room with deep plush sofas and tables laden with interesting books and magazines. In winter, roaring log fires fill the room with life while guests partake of afternoon tea. The elegant dining room features a 15 foot solid oak table.

Three impeccably furnished, comfortable, light and airy bedrooms have lovely views over the three acre garden which leads to two beautiful trout lakes (four and five acres) and woodland. Fishing is available to guests.

The Hosts

Nigel, an arable and livestock farmer, and Elizabeth both enjoy all aspects of country living. Having lived here all their lives, they possess good local knowledge and are only too happy to advise on the more unusual places to visit.

The Location

Halfway between Stratford-upon-Avon and Oxford, 22 miles from Cheltenham, 5 from Stow-on-the-Wold and 11 from Blenheim Palace, makes Rectory Farm an ideal centre for touring the Cotswolds. Warwick Castle, Chastleton and Rousham Houses, Hidcote and Bourton House Gardens are within easy reach. There is something for everybody, including a popular walk from the house to the Rollright Stones (a Bronze Age stone circle).

Nigel & Elizabeth Colston
Rectory Farm
Salford, Chipping Norton,
Oxfordshire, OX7 5YY
Tel: 01608 643209 or 07866 834208
enquiries@rectoryfarm.info
www.rectoryfarm.info   5991

Finding Us

Salford is one mile north-west of Chipping Norton off the A44. Rectory Farm is at the far end of the village. Go past the Black Horse pub, left at the telephone box (Cooks Lane), up the hill, past the children's play area on your right and then left into the farm drive. Continue for 200 yards through the avenue of trees, and turn left into the house and gardens.

Rooms (per person per night incl. breakfast)

1 King Size (5') Room (en suite)	**£46-£55**
1 Super King (6')/Twin Room (private)	**£46-£55**
1 Super King (6')/Twin Room (en suite)	**£46-£55**
Single Supplement	**£15-£25**

Meals

Breakfast only

Opening Times

Closed 1st December - 1st February

Payment Options

Facilities & Services

Rosemary Grove-White
Home Farmhouse, Charlton,
Nr Banbury, Oxfordshire OX17 3DR
Tel: 01295 811683 or 07795 207000
Fax: 01295 811683
grovewhite@lineone.net
www.homefarmhouse.co.uk   4998

The Property

Home Farmhouse, Charlton is nearly 500 years old and retains many of its original features – beams, inglenook fireplaces and winding staircases. Most important of all, though, is the feeling of friendliness and warmth which many guests remark on when they enter the house for the first time. The house itself could not be more conveniently laid out for guests with three charming bedrooms each enjoying its own approach staircase and en suite bathroom. The bedrooms have extremely comfortable beds made up traditionally with sheets, blankets and eiderdown and are provided with television and radio, fresh fruit, chocolates and flapjacks.

Tea and cake are offered to guests on arrival – in the delightful walled garden if the weather permits or in the attractive drawing room if it does not or if the garden is closed under the NGS scheme. Breakfast, to order the night before, including homemade bread, jams and blackberry and apple compote from the garden, is served in the elegant dining room and is usually a lively talkative affair with Nigel's military ancestors looking down approvingly from the walls.

The Hosts

Nigel, Rosemary and Goliath and Samson, two miniature wire haired dachshunds, offer the friendliest welcome. Nigel retired to become Chief Executive of the British Horse Society, prior to which, he spent 32 years in the Army. Rosemary trained as an interior designer and for thirty years has very successfully run her own interior design, soft furnishing and upholstery business.

The Location

From this tranquil setting, you are perfectly placed to enjoy Oxford, Stratford-upon-Avon, Warwick Castle, Blenheim Palace, Waddesdon Manor and Hidcote. Beautiful Cotswold villages such as Chipping Campden, Broadway, Snowshill and the Slaughters are just a stone's throw away and Silverstone Grand Prix, Blenheim Horse Trials and Bicester Village are all close by. There is a good friendly pub just 100 yards away – reservation recommended.

Finding Us

South: leave the M40 at junction 10; follow the A43 towards Northampton. After 5 miles turn left to Charlton. On entering the village turn left down the village street; 100 yards after the pub, turn left into a gravelled lane. From north, leave M40 at Banbury, junction 11; turn left onto A422. After 4½ miles at Farthinghoe turn right to Charlton. Straight down the village street and turn left into gravelled lane 100 yards after the pub.

Rooms   (per person per night incl. breakfast)

1 King Size (5') Room (en suite)	**£47**
2 Super King (6') /Twin Rooms (en suite)	**£47**
Single Supplement	**£18**

Meals

Supper	**£22**
Dinner	**£28**

(Both by prior arrangement; min 4 persons)

Opening Times

Closed Christmas

Payment Options

Facilities & Services

John & Sally Wass
Holmby House
Sibford Ferris, Nr Banbury
Oxfordshire OX15 5RG
Tel: 01295 780104 or 07968 158598
Fax: 01295 780104
sally.wass@btinternet.com
www.holmbyhouse.com   4994

Finding Us

Exit M40, J11, go towards Banbury. At 3rd roundabout (Tesco ahead) left onto Southam Rd. At Banbury Cross roundabout, right onto B4035. After Swalcliffe, at top of hill, left to Sibford Ferris. Straight over, into village. Holmby House is first house on right.

Rooms   (per person per night incl. breakfast)

2 Super King (6')/Twin Rooms (en suite)	**£45-£55**
1 King Size (5') Room (en suite)	**£40-£50**
1 Double (4'6") Room (en suite)	**£40-£50**
1 Super King (6') Room (private)	**£45-£55**
Single Supplement	**£15-£20**

Meals

Dinner   £35

Opening Times

Open all year

Payment Options

£ C € ◯ VISA ◯

Facilities & Services

[icons]

The Property

Surrounded by views of undulating countryside and on the edge of a small Oxfordshire village, sits Holmby House. An impressive drive leads to a wisteria clad, elegant Victorian house. On arrival, guests are welcomed with tea and homemade cakes in front of a log fire in the winter or on the terrace in the summer. Inside, the recently restored house is luxuriously decorated with classic fabrics and antique furniture. Bedrooms are spacious and light with fantastic views. Guests are greeted in their rooms by an array of facilities including large comfortable beds, good sized baths or power showers, television, telephone, fresh flowers, a bowl of fruit and bottled mineral water.

The garden is a colourful, fragrant oasis and includes a secluded summer house. For the more active guest, there is an outdoor heated pool, tennis court and croquet lawn.

The Hosts

Sociable and enthusiastic hosts, Sally and John enjoy sharing their home and entertaining. Sally, an ex-Barts ward sister and past England lacrosse player, enjoys all aspects of country living. An aficionado of Claire Macdonald, guests are assured of good cooking from local produce and home grown vegetables. John is a hormone specialist and has a particular interest in wine. Your hosts are keen on opera, theatre and travel - especially to Scotland.

The Location

On the edge of the Cotswolds, there is something for everyone near Holmby House. Stratford-upon-Avon, Stow on the Wold, Chipping Campden, Oxford and Warwick are all within a short distance of the property. There are excellent walking and cycling opportunities not far from the doorstep with golf and horse riding available locally. The village has a number of good pubs and a new, highly rated restaurant.

The Property

Splendidly set in 400 acres of the unspoilt Teme Valley, this elegant Georgian farmhouse looking south over the river towards the Wigmore Rolls, offers sophisticated hospitality in beautiful relaxed surroundings. A large, mature garden, a masterpiece in light and shade, is brimming with unusual herbaceous plants, flourishing lilies and hostas around a 12th century motte, ha-ha and millstream.

Guests are cosseted in this genteel three storey gentleman's residence, with well proportioned and attractively decorated rooms, containing beautiful antiques and paintings, collected over many years. Elegant bedrooms, with the emphasis on comfortable furnishings, have beautiful cotton appliqué sheets and pillowcases on the lovely beds and en suite or private bathrooms, complete with special finishing touches.

The Hosts

Hayden and Yvonne have been farming at Upper Buckton for over three decades. They have a wide knowledge and love of the surrounding countryside and enjoy introducing their guests to this unspoilt part of the Welsh Borders. They are warm hosts who endeavour to make guests feel immediately relaxed and at home in their haven of peace, good humour and great food. Yvonne's cooking is an imaginative and sophisticated blend of traditional and Cordon Bleu cooking. Hayden takes great care over the wine list, which features the best European and New World wines.

The Location

Visitors will find many interesting places to visit including Ludlow, Much Wenlock, the Black and White Villages of Herefordshire, the Castles: Ludlow, Powis, Croft and Stokesey and National Trust properties and gardens galore. There are many walks in the area and horse riding can be arranged locally. Stabling available to bring your own horse.

Hayden & Yvonne Lloyd
Upper Buckton, Leintwardine,
Craven Arms, Shropshire SY7 0JU
Tel: 01547 540634
Fax: 01547 540634
ghlloydco@btconnect.com
www.upperbuckton.co.uk   5984

Finding Us

From Ludlow take A49 north towards Shrewsbury. At Bromfield turn left, A4113 to Knighton. Pass through Leintwardine continuing on A4113 to Walford. Turn right into narrow road signed Buckton. Upper Buckton is in the hamlet of Buckton, third house on the left. Please drive into courtyard.

Rooms (per person per night incl. breakfast)

1 Super King (6') Room (en suite)	£48-£55
1 Super King (6')/Twin Room (en suite)	£48-£55
1 Super King (6')/Twin Room (private)	£48-£55
Single Supplement	£15

Meals

Dinner	£30

Opening Times

Closed Occasionally

Payment Options

Facilities & Services

Charlotte & Kevin Dowd
Hambrook House
13 Kennedy Road, Shrewsbury
Shropshire SY3 7AD
Tel: 01743 365456
charlotte@hambrookhouse.co.uk
www.hambrookhouse.co.uk   5939

Finding Us
Detailed directions available at time of booking.

Rooms (per person per night incl. breakfast)

4 King Size (5') Rooms	(en suite)	**£50-£60**
1 Double (4'6") Room	(en suite)	**£47.50**
1 Twin (2 x 3') Room	(en suite)	**£55**
Single Occupancy		**£80-£105**

Meals
Breakfast Only

Opening Times
Closed Christmas

Payment Options

Facilities & Services

The Property

Just a beautiful ten minute walk from the centre of Shrewsbury, Hambrook House is a stunning Victorian Villa located in Shrewsbury's most elegant residential area. It has been lovingly restored with many original features including Minton tiles, fine stained glass windows and cast iron fireplaces. With plenty of off street parking, Hambrook House is an ideal place to stay if visiting this historic county town of Shropshire. It is also popular with visitors to nearby Shrewsbury School.

Reception rooms are extremely comfortable, with lovely antique furniture and paintings to enjoy. A guest sitting room with views of the garden has a piano for anyone wishing to 'tickle the ivories'! Bedrooms are all refurbished to a very high standard, with pocket sprung mattresses, quality white bed linen, towels and toiletries. All have en suite bath or shower, tea and coffee making facilities, large HD flat screen television and free WiFi. For the less mobile guest there are two ground floor rooms, one with walk-in shower.

Breakfast is served at individual tables in the bright and airy dining room, and produce is locally sourced, with free-range eggs, sausages, bacon and Pimhill Muesli.

The Hosts

Charlotte and Kevin moved to Shrewsbury with their young family a few years ago, and since opening have rapidly developed an excellent reputation. Kevin is a chartered surveyor and Charlotte had a career in publishing. They are always happy to advise visitors on restaurants, hostelries and other places to visit just a short stroll away.

The Location

With over 600 listed buildings, Shrewsbury is a historic and vibrant market town with a splendid medieval heritage. A veritable 'shopper's paradise' it boasts many independent businesses. It is the perfect base to explore the museums and historic sites of Ironbridge Gorge and the awe-inspiring aqueducts of Pontcysyllte and Chirk.

The Property

Wollaston Lodge is an early Victorian former hunting lodge and is a perfect example of contemporary style, cleverly combined with classic architecture and features, resulting in a superb luxury home. Situated in immaculate Italianate landscaped gardens, complete with topiary and splendid views, there are terraces where guests can enjoy tea on arrival on warmer days, and play tennis, if inclined.

Recently thoroughly restored, the interior exudes style while retaining original qualities. Spacious rooms, high ceilings, subtle colour schemes and comfort abound in this haven of tranquillity that we know will be loved by Wolsey Lodge aficionados.

Generously proportioned bedrooms (one with a four poster bed) are individually furnished to an excellent standard, with fine linens and en suite bath/shower rooms. Delicious breakfasts, and dinners by prior arrangement, are served in the orangery, overlooking the garden. The blueberry pancakes and eggs Benedict are legendary!

The Hosts

Sandy and Grant love entertaining and they have certainly discovered their métier. Nothing is too much trouble when looking after guests and they are always pleased to recommend many superb places to eat out locally. They have run a number of businesses together over the years, many involving gardening and garden products – hence the fantastic grounds of their home! Their grown up children have fled the nest and they now share their home with friendly dog Lara (who welcomes accompanying guests on walks!), and Spiro the cat.

The Location

On the Welsh border and ideal for exploring the nearby market town of Shrewsbury, a medieval paradise of alleys, bars, restaurants and independent shops. For the more culturally minded, National Trust properties abound, plus museums, theatre, and galleries - even a Tudor cinema! Popular with walkers, horticulturists and race-goers, it is within easy reach of the coast.

Sandy & Grant Williams
Wollaston Lodge
Wollaston
Halfway House
Shrewsbury
Shropshire SY5 9DN
Tel: 01743 884831 & 07736 152392
enjoylife@wollastonlodge.co.uk
www.wollastonlodge.co.uk   5936

Finding Us

From Shrewsbury Ring Road take A458 Welshpool road, travel 8 miles then take right turn signed Wollaston. Wollaston Lodge is first house on left. From Welshpool take A458, 2 miles after Middletown turn left signed Wollaston. Many satellite navigation systems will take you on an unnecessary detour.

Rooms   (per person per night incl. breakfast)

2 King Size (5') Rooms (en suite)	**£47.50**
1 Family Room with 1 King Size (5') & Twin (2 x 3') Room (Private)	**£55**
Single Supplement	**£27.50**

Meals

Dinner (3 courses) (By prior arrangement)	**£30**

Opening Times

Open all year

Payment Options

Facilities & Services

Martin & Frances Hardman
Pitfour House
High Street, Timsbury,
Bath, Somerset BA2 0HT
Tel: 01761 479554
pitfourhouse@btinternet.com
www.pitfourhouse.co.uk   5976

Finding Us

Take A367 from Bath to Radstock and Wells. After 3 miles turn right onto B3115 (Timsbury and Tunley). Continue for 4 miles to Timsbury. Turn left after shops into Newmans Lane, bearing right into the High Street. Pitfour House is 50 yards on the right.

The Property

Splendid food, convivial company and truly wonderful hospitality are to be found at Pitfour House, a quintessentially English experience in a charming Georgian home, which boasts a beautiful staircase and cupola. Situated in the rural village of Timsbury just outside Bath, the house, which stands back from the High Street, has a wonderfully mellow stone façade, glimpsed beyond large gates.

Tea and home made delicacies are served on arrival, after which guests may enjoy the comforts of an elegantly furnished formal sitting room with open fire. There is another separate, and more relaxed sitting room with television, and a delightful panelled dining room where guests dine superbly in the company of their hosts. Being of typical 18th century proportions, the house also offers well appointed, comfortable bedrooms with king size Vi-Spring beds, one with an en suite shower room and the other with its own adjacent bathroom.

The main ½ acre walled garden is to the rear of the property and is stocked with mature shrubs and trees, a productive greenhouse and a thriving vegetable garden.

The Hosts

Martin is a retired paediatrician and enjoys gardening and furniture restoration. Frances is a retired dentist and is a keen flower arranger. They both enjoy entertaining and the challenge of providing good quality food using home grown produce whenever possible.

The Location

Timsbury is an interesting rural village with many scenic walks nearby. Bath is within an easy drive, with the great advantage of a Park & Ride just 4 miles from the house. Other places of interest include the cathedral city of Wells, Glastonbury, Tyntesfield and SS Great Britain in Bristol.

Rooms (per person per night incl. breakfast)

2 Super King (6')/Twin Rooms (1 en suite/1 private)	**£45-£50**
Single Supplement	**£25**

A supplement may be charged for a single night at a weekend

Meals

Dinner	2 courses	**£28.50**
	3 courses	**£36**

Opening Times

Closed Occasionally

Payment Options

Facilities & Services

The Property
A precious gem in a perfect setting, it is as if time has stood still at Beryl, a beautiful small Gothic mansion standing serenely in 13 acres of parkland, one mile north east of magnificent Wells Cathedral.

Designed and built in 1838, by Benjamin Ferry, a pupil of Pugin, Beryl has been lovingly restored with Gothic inspired features and a wealth of fine antiques. The elegant drawing room is the perfect place to unwind in luxurious style; the green room is perfect for watching television, playing board games and enjoying a much needed drink. Wells offers excellent dining opportunities from relaxed pubs to upmarket restaurants.

Individually decorated, well appointed bedrooms enjoy views of the cathedral and gardens where an outdoor pool, croquet lawn, restored walled garden, woodland area and a children's play area are waiting to tempt guests outside in all seasons.

The Hosts
Holly and her daughter Mary-Ellen continue a tradition of gracious hospitality, started with her late husband in 1980. They share an eye for fine detail, and a complete understanding of how guests love to be treated is evident in this warm and welcoming home.

Guests can enjoy a lovely jewellery boutique run by Mary-Ellen and her husband Edward Byworth in the Coach House.

The Location
At the foot of the Mendips, Beryl is perfect for West Country touring. Wells, the smallest city in Europe and home to its oldest inhabited street is only a mile away. Wookey Hole, Cheddar Caves, Longleat Country House, Stourhead and Montacute House are all within easy reach, with Weston-Super-Mare, Bath and Bristol a little further afield.

Holly Nowell & Mary-Ellen Nowell
Beryl, Top of Hawkers Lane, Wells,
Somerset BA5 3JP
Tel: 01749 678738   Fax: 01749 670508
stay@beryl-wells.co.uk
www.beryl-wells.co.uk   5995

Finding Us
Leave or approach Wells on Radstock Road B3139. Follow signs to the Horringtons, opposite BP garage turn left into Hawkers Lane (not Beryl Lane) next to bus stop. Drive to top of lane - see sign 'Beryl' - continue up leafy drive, approximately 300 yards to main gate.

Rooms (per person per night incl. breakfast)

4 Super King (6')/Twin Rooms (en suite)	£55-£80
1 Super King (6') Four Poster Room (en suite)	£80
2 King Size (5') Rooms (en suite)	£57.50-£65
2 King Size (5') Four Poster Rooms (en suite)	£65
1 Twin (2 x 3'6") Room (en suite)	£72.50
Single Supplement	£30

Chair lift to first floor

Meals
Breakfast only

Opening Times
Closed Christmas

Payment Options

Facilities & Services

The Property

Sweep up the drive to this imposing early eighteenth century farmhouse, set in beautiful Somerset countryside, where you will receive a warm welcome. Michael and Lavinia lovingly restored the house and filled it with beautiful antiques, paintings, porcelain and sumptuous fabrics, which all create a serene atmosphere.

Bedrooms are light, elegant and individually styled, with supremely comfortable beds and quality white linen. They all have uninterrupted long views of the surrounding countryside, with the Stourhead Forest in the distance, little changed since the eighteenth century. The matching pretty bathrooms have everything guests could wish for.

On sunny days enjoy the now mature garden, created from a field, or in the winter, the elegant drawing room with a blazing fire, an abundance of books, and perfect peace and tranquility.

The Hosts

Michael and Lavinia are charming and easy, and offer good food, good company and a relaxed and friendly atmosphere. Michael has published seventeen military history books. Lavinia, a Cordon Bleu cook, ensures that dining is a highlight of your stay. She uses local ingredients from local producers and vegetables from the garden. They have a keen interest in history, and enjoy sharing local knowledge of this stunning area.

The Location

The property is set in an Area of Outstanding Natural Beauty and is close to Bath, Salisbury and Wells, It is surrounded by a wealth of classic English gardens and great houses such as Stourhead, Montacute, Longleat, Lytes Carey and Barrington Court. Wincanton Racecourse is close by. Glastonbury Tor, Cheddar Gorge, the Mendips and the Somerset Levels are a short distance away.

Michael & Lavinia Dewar
Rectory Farm House
Charlton Musgrove, Wincanton
Somerset BA9 8ET
Tel: 01963 34599
l.dewar@btconnect.com
www.rectoryfarmhouse.com   5971

Finding Us

From East: Exit A303 at B3081 for Blandford Forum & Shaftesbury. Go under A303, left at T-junction, right after Hunters Lodge Pub, signed Charlton Musgrove. Go 1 mile and left into Rectory Lane. After 0.4 miles Rectory Farm House is on right. Follow drive to the yard to park.

Rooms (per person per night incl. breakfast)

1 Super King (6') Room (en suite)	£55
1 Super King (6')/ Twin Room (private)	£50
Single Supplement	£20

Meals

Dinner	£35
Supper	£25

Opening Times

Closed Christmas & New Year

Payment Options

Facilities & Services

Chris & Maggie Knight
The Old Vicarage
Church Street
Castle Cary
Somerset BA7 7EJ
Tel: 01963 350226
mcknightcm@btopenworld.com   **5949**

Finding Us

In Castle Cary continue through the town towards Yeovil (B3152). On your right pass the garage and at All Saints Church turn right into drive which is on the far side of and adjacent to the churchyard.

Rooms (per person per night incl. breakfast)

1 King Size (5') Damask Room (en suite)	**£60**
1 King Size (5') Silk Room (en suite)	**£60**
Single Supplement	**£15**

Meals

Dinner	**£25-£30**
(By prior arrangement)	

Opening Times

Closed Christmas & New Year

Payment Options

Facilities & Services

The Property

The Old Vicarage is in the historic market town of Castle Cary but although in the centre of town and an easy walk to shops, its setting is one of utter peace and tranquillity, just one of the qualities that make this home so special.

Elegantly furnished, the large dining and drawing rooms and the stunning two storey conservatory, where guests can relax, provide pleasurable views over the two acres of garden with its sweeping lawns, graceful trees and old stone walls and courtyard. The swimming pool and surrounding terrace with its vine covered pergola provide another treat for guests to enjoy – what a joy at the end of a day's sightseeing.

Each guest room has been carefully decorated and furnished with gorgeous fabrics, paintings and interesting artefacts. Beds are king size and bathrooms have both a tub and separate shower. Taking breakfast from the extensive menu - choose from full English, fish or the vegetarian option - will leave you perfectly set for the day; and dinner will be another gastronomic delight as Maggie is an outstanding cook.

The Hosts

Maggie and Chris are easy-going company and make their guests feel immediately welcome and relaxed. Together they have lived in America, India, Bermuda and Scotland before settling in Somerset. Chris was formerly a lawyer and magistrate and Maggie, a nurse and teacher.

The Location

Castle Cary borders the beautiful county of Dorset, perfect for a stop-off en route to or from Devon and Cornwall as well an ideal base to explore Somerset - Wells with its stunning Cathedral, Longleat, the world famous Hauser and Wirth Gallery in Bruton, Haynes Motor Museum, Fleet Air Arm Museum, Wincanton Racecourse, Glastonbury Tor and Abbey, as well as many National Trust properties including Montacute House and Stourhead.

Frances and Tim Meeres Young
Stoberry House
Stoberry Park, Wells, Somerset BA5 3LD
Tel: 01749 672906
stay@stoberry-park.co.uk
www.stoberryhouse.co.uk   5955

Finding Us

From Bristol or Bath enter Wells on A39; immediately after 30mph sign turn left into College Road, then left through wrought iron gateway into Stoberry Park. At top of park bear right and follow tar driveway into walled garden.

Rooms (per person per night incl. breakfast)

1 Super King (6')/Twin Room (en suite)	£47.50-£55
1 King Size (5') Four Poster Room (en suite)	£57.50-£67.50
1 King Size (5') Room (en suite)	£47.50-£55
1 Single (4'6") Room (en suite)	£65-£75
Garden Studio, Super King (6')/Twin Room (en suite)	£62.50-£72.50
Single Supplement	£35

Cooked breakfast on request with small supplement
Reduced rates for 2 or 3 night stays.

Meals

Light Supper	£9.50
Supper (2 courses)	£22.50-£25
Dinner (3 courses)	£27.50-£32.50

(Supper & Dinner by prior arrangement and for a minimum of 6 persons)

Opening Times

Open all year

Payment Options

Facilities & Services

The Property

On a hillside, set in 25 acres of parkland, Stoberry House offers everything expected from a traditional Wolsey Lodge - and more! With breathtaking, panoramic views over the city of Wells and the surrounding area, it is a short walk to the city centre.

The spectacular garden, which has featured in magazines, has sculptures integrated as works of art and floodlit at night, was designed by owner Frances to provide year-round colour and is filled with magnificent plants, ponds, a box maze, paths and hidden seating areas where guests relax in peace and tranquillity.

Inside, this comfortable house is stylish furnished with family antiques and beautiful mementoes of their travels. Bedrooms and bathrooms have luxurious robes, slippers and handmade toiletries, and guests can also relax in the drawing room, television room or their own reading room.

Breakfast is Continental, with fresh fruit and juices, delicious breads and jams, pastries, hams and cheeses, or a cooked breakfast is available on request for a small supplement. There are many excellent restaurants nearby or, by prior arrangement, light suppers or gourmet dinners are available, with a very extensive wine list.

The Hosts

Frances has a background in hospitality, and it shows! Tim is an international water engineering consultant and they have travelled extensively. Frances catered commercially and now enjoys showcasing her formidable culinary prowess and love of entertaining to provide their guests with a truly memorable stay.

The Location

So much to see and do! The wonderful city of Wells, the Cathedral, the Bishops Palace and Gardens, Open Market and Vicar's Close are all just a walk away. Wookey Hole Caves, Cheddar Gorge, Glastonbury Abbey and Glastonbury Tor are not to be missed. There are also many excellent walks around Wells and the Quantocks.

The Property

Bordering the Exmoor National Park, close to the sea, stands what is quite simply, a special Wolsey Lodge. Nestled amidst the trees, Glen Lodge is a tranquil haven in a picture perfect setting. Built in 1886, the original features have been blended into the warm and welcoming home of Meryl and David Salter.

Set in 21 acres, gardens extend all around tiers with a captivating stream cascading over waterfalls alongside secluded terraces, the croquet lawn and seating areas to while away your time or workout in the gym. Exmoor and the coastal paths lead directly from the gardens and the village of Porlock, with its array of shops and tea rooms, is just a short stroll away.

This is a home to relax in and the cosy library, outdoor Jacuzzi hot tub, sitting and dining rooms all enjoy the amazing views across the garden to the sea beyond. Tea and cakes are served every afternoon of your stay and are well worth returning home for! Each bedroom has been carefully furnished with all of the finishing touches you would expect of a Wolsey Lodge and your breakfast here will be nothing less than exceptional – the freshly baked muffins are a particular speciality and not to be missed.

The Hosts

David is a master craftsman. When at home the garden is his domain and he is a keen sailor and birdwatcher. Meryl is an outstanding cook and keen photographer as well as sharing 'twitching' with David.

The Location

Exmoor is a delight throughout the year – don't miss a walk to Dunkery beacon, charming Porlock Weir, Valley of the Rocks, cliff railway at Lynton, Dunster Castle, Tarr Steps and of course the Exmoor ponies and deer. Take a stroll across the open moors before enjoying a meal and drink at one of the wonderful pubs in the area.

Meryl and David Salter
Glen Lodge
Hawkcombe, Porlock,
Somerset TA24 8LN
Tel: 01643 863371 or 07786 118933
Fax: 01643 863016
glenlodge@gmail.com
www.glenlodge.net   5950

Finding Us

On entering Porlock, turn left at church onto Parsons Street; approximately ½ mile turn left over bridge. Gate to Glen Lodge is directly ahead.

Rooms (per person per night incl. breakfast)

1 King Size (5') Room (en suite)	**£47.50-£55**
1 King Size (5') Room (private)	**£47.50-£55**
2 Double (4'6") Rooms (en suite)	**£47.50-£55**
1 Twin (2 x 3') Room (private)	**£47.50-£55**
Single Supplement	£17

Meals

Supper (2 courses)	£23
Dinner (3 courses)	£34

Opening Times

Closed Christmas & New Year

Payment Options

Facilities & Services

The Property

This beautifully converted 100 year old barn is on the edge of the quiet village of South Barrow, just off the A303, with views of the ancient site of Camelot – reputedly King Arthur's fortress. The guest suite at this modern and spacious Wolsey Lodge is elegantly furnished and offers a choice of either a twin or double bedded room with a private bathroom.

There is a large guest sitting room where guests are welcomed on arrival, with a dining area at one end to enjoy a full English breakfast with views from the French windows over the expansive gardens. Wood burning stoves and under floor heating throughout add extra comfort.

Along the front of the barn is a lawn edged with shrubs and with tables and chairs where guests can relax. The barn is all on one level and could be ideal for the less mobile.

Dog owners are welcome, usually greeted by Berty, the resident Labrador. Keen riders wanting to explore the area can stable their mounts at the neighbouring equestrian centre.

The Hosts

Jenny and Peter are enthusiastic sailors and keep an ocean-going yacht at Portland. Jenny spent much of her life in Africa, including Ghana and Tanzania but returned to the UK to educate her teenage daughter. Peter has enjoyed a long career as a television drama director and producer.

Both enjoy cooking and offer a delicious dinner by arrangement. Alternatively they are pleased to recommend nearby restaurants and pubs and organise taxis.

The Location

Being so handy for the A303, South Barrow is ideal for travellers. Between Wincanton (with its famous racecourse), Yeovil and Sherborne, it is also the perfect spot for exploring the South Somerset/Dorset area or heading south to the World Heritage Jurassic Coast. Alternatively one can venture north to Bristol and Bath via Shepton Mallet.

Jenny Cox & Peter Jefferies
The Church Byres
South Barrow
Yeovil
Somerset BA22 7LN
Tel: 07765 175058
bookings@somerset-bb.co.uk
www.somerset-bb.co.uk   2949

Finding Us

Enter village of South Barrow from Sparkford. Pass South Barrow Church on right. Then down a hollow and approach an s-bend in road. On the s-bend turn sharp right up small lane. 100 yards on turn sharp right up gravel drive. Half way up drive park in small parking bay which is directly opposite french windows - your entrance.

Rooms   (per person per night incl. breakfast)

1 Double (4'6") or Twin (2 x 3')   **£40-£50**
Room (private)

Single Supplement   **£10**

Meals

Dinner   (4 Courses)   **£30**
(By prior arrangement)

Opening Times

Closed Christmas

Payment Options

Facilities & Services

The Property

A stunning, Grade I listed luxury Georgian town house, a short walk from the city centre in one of Bath's foremost crescents. On a quiet hillside with panoramic views of Bath, the Crescent looks out across a field, complete with grazing sheep, offering guests a rare contemporary taste of Georgian life plus a rural experience in an urban setting.

This six storey family home has been lovingly restored into a fabulous bed and breakfast establishment, keeping original features – including its own torch snuffer outside and its coach house.

The three bedrooms are extremely spacious and individual. Each has its own private bathroom, complete with roll top bath. The basement room even has its own snooker room with full sized table. There are glorious views of the city and the lovely 100 foot garden, which guests may enjoy when the weather allows. Elegant drawing and withdrawing rooms are available to relax in and on-street parking can be arranged.

The Hosts

Rebecca and Robert turned their family home into a bed and breakfast a few years ago when their daughters 'fled the nest'. Robert is a lawyer and Rebecca a professional reflexologist. They are extremely charming and welcoming hosts and are always happy to provide personal recommendations for local pubs and restaurants and make reservations if needed. Rebecca's delicious cooked breakfasts, complete with freshly squeezed orange juice and homemade preserves will set you up for the day.

The Location

Designated a World Heritage site, Bath itself is unique and the only place in Britain with naturally hot spa water. England's most complete Georgian architecture, iconic visitor attractions, museums, fabulous boutique shops, street theatre, festivals and everything else this exciting city offers is but a short stroll away. The area surrounding Bath is steeped with gardens, historic houses and other tourist attractions.

Robert & Rebecca Derry-Evans
17 Lansdown Crescent
Bath
Somerset
BA1 5EX
Tel: 01225 471741 or 07802 416969
derries@globalnet.co.uk   **5937**
www.bedandbreakfastbathuk.co.uk

Finding Us

Detailed directions available at time of booking.

Rooms (per person per night incl. breakfast)

2 King Size (5') Rooms (private)	**£55-£65**
1 Double (4'6") Room (private)	**£50-£60**
Single Supplement	**£35**

Meals

Breakfast only

Opening Times

Closed Christmas & New Year

Payment Options

Facilities & Services

The Property

Set against the backdrop of the beautiful Peak District National Park is a gem of a Wolsey Lodge offering the peace and relaxation only found deep in countryside such as that around Martinslow Farm. Throughout the year the welcome is wonderfully warm with stunning view to lift your spirits in all seasons.

Over 250 years old and Grade II listed, Martinslow Farm was once a donkey station serving the local lead mining industry and today is the comfortable home of Diana and Richard Bloor. It is the perfect location for exploring the Peak District.

In the main house oak beamed rooms with stone floors are comfortably furnished for maximum relaxation whilst across in the stable block, the bedrooms are wonderfully warm with hot water aplenty to rest tired bodies at the end a day's exploring. The two en suite guest rooms, one double and one twin, can be interconnected making them perfect for a family or group of friends. Dinner, if you choose to eat in, and breakfast is delicious and focuses on local produce wherever possible. Being 1000ft above sea level the views from Martinslow Farm are spectacular on a clear day and the garden is surrounded by eight acres of grounds for guests to enjoy.

The Hosts

Diana is a retired physiotherapist and whilst Richard retired from his family's shoe business he is now an accident investigator. They both share a love of the countryside and walking their dogs around the area but above all they truly enjoy entertaining guests in their relaxing and informal home.

The Location

The Peak District is a walkers and cyclists paradise. Close by are Wedgewood Museum, Pottery Museum, Chatsworth House, Haddon Hall, Hardwick Hall, Keddleston Hall and Sudbury Hall.

Richard & Diana Bloor
Martinslow Farm
Winkhill
Leek
Staffordshire ST13 7PZ
Tel: 01538 304500
richard.bloor@btclick.com
www.martinslowfarm.co.uk   5941

Finding Us

In the centre of Winkhill take sign to Grindon, carry on up steep, narrow lane until you can go no further (ignore crossroads half way up lane). Turn left at triangle junction, the house is 250 yards on right set below the lane.

Rooms (per person per night incl. breakfast)

1 King Size (5') Room	(en suite)	**£50**
1 Twin (2 x 3') Room	(en suite)	**£50**
Single Supplement		**£20**

Minimum 2 night stay November to February

Meals

Dinner (3 courses)	**£37**
Supper (2 courses)	**£28**
Light Supper	**£15**

Opening Times

Closed Christmas

Payment Options

Facilities & Services

Jeffrey & Caroline Bowden
Haughley House
Haughley
Suffolk IP14 3NS
Tel: 01449 673398 or 07860 284722
bowden@keme.co.uk
www.haughleyhouse.co.uk   3982

The Property

Set in the historical surroundings of a small village in the heart of Suffolk, the imposing timber framed Haughley House is a late medieval manor.

Inside the manor there is a sumptuous mix of high quality Georgian furniture and exquisite silk lined walls. Antique weapons, fans and plates add to the country house style of a more leisurely age. Guests will be offered tea and home made cakes upon arrival.

All three guest bedrooms are in the oldest part of the house and original oak beams are visible in all three. Both double rooms have period beds (including a majestic mahogany four poster) and en suite shower, whilst the twin room has en suite bath and shower. The comfortable sitting room offers a quiet retreat all year round and a log fire burns in winter.

Outside, the three acre garden has well stocked flower beds and guests can relax in the shade of the ancient Cedar of Lebanon and magnificent beech tree. The orchard and walled kitchen garden provides virtually all the vegetables for the house, whilst the host's own flock of hens provide eggs for the table and their stock provides beef and game for the guests.

The Hosts

Jeffrey is Lord of the Manor and was once a cavalry officer before running a commercial business in London. He and his wife Caroline are keenly interested in hunting, shooting, food and wine. All food is prepared using only the finest ingredients and cooked on the Aga.

The Location

The manor is set within a conservation village with a traditional pub. Within 15 minutes of Haughley is the Georgian market town of Bury St Edmunds, 30 minutes to Cambridge and other historical villages and 45 minutes to the heritage coast.

Finding Us

From the A14, leave at Junction 49. As you proceed up the village street, take the left fork at the village green; Haughley House will be found 100 yards on left hand side.

Rooms (per person per night incl. breakfast)

1 Double (4'6") Room (en suite)	**£50**
1 King Size (5') Room (en suite)	**£60**
1 Twin (2 x 3') Room (en suite)	**£60**
Single Occupancy	**£65-£75**

Meals

Supper	**£18**
Dinner	**£32**

Opening Times

Closed occasionally

Payment Options

£ C € [cards] VISA

Facilities & Services

[icons] WiFi [icons]

Andrew & Eileen Gilbert
West Stow Hall
Icklingham Road, West Stow
Bury St Edmunds, Suffolk IP28 6EY
Tel: 01284 728127
eileengilbert54@aol.com
www.weststowhall.com   3961

Finding Us

From M11 take A11 towards Mildenhall. Before Mildenhall, take A1101 to Bury St Edmunds, after 3 miles turn left to West Stow, on entering village West Stow Hall clearly marked on left and on same road as the Anglo Saxon Village, so follow the signs.

The Property

Take a step back in time into the historic and stunning West Stow Hall. A Grade I listed Tudor house, renovated in the 1840's and now home to Eileen and Andy Gilbert who have made it a perfect B&B retreat. Walk through the ancient Gatehouse and the colonnade linking it to the main house to be greeted by the family dogs and afternoon tea. Spend a while marveling at the magnificent inglenook fireplace – reputedly the largest in Suffolk - and absorbing the history around you.

There are large guest rooms in the main house and in the garden there is a studio which, with its ground floor access, is ideally suited for less mobile guests. Each room is light, spacious and furnished with great care to ensure your stay is simply as comfortable as possible. A good night's sleep is followed by breakfast featuring an array of fine, local fayre.

The gardens feature lavender lined paths, colourful flowers, an orchard and small woods. As well as being child friendly, guests can, by arrangement, bring their dogs for a small charge if staying in the Studio. Nearby restaurants and pubs offer a wide choice for dining.

The Hosts

Andy, a lawyer, commutes into the City every day whilst Eileen was a teacher. Andy's interest in all things steam is evident in the splendid engines parked in the driveway which he enjoys showing to guests. Eileen is a good cook and enjoys welcoming and looking after her guests.

The Location

Historic Bury St Edmunds is a great base for exploring. West Stow Anglo Saxon Village, Ely Cathedral, Fullers Mill Gardens, Newmarket racing and Cambridge are all within easy reach along with the National Trust properties Anglesey Abbey and Ickworth House. Trout fishing, golfing, walking and cycling are great pastimes for holiday makers staying here.

Rooms (per person per night incl. breakfast)

2 King Size (5') Rooms (en suite)	£55-£60
1 Super King (6')/ Twin Room (en suite)	£55-£60
1 Double (4'6") Studio Room (en suite)	£55-£60
Single Supplement	£15-£20

Meals

Supper	£20
Dinner	£35
(Both by prior arrangement)	

Opening Times

Closed Christmas

Payment Options

Facilities & Services

The Property

This former rectory, nestling within the Broads and with views over the Waveney Valley, is situated in an elevated position on the Norfolk/Suffolk border between Beccles and Bungay and within the Ellingham Mill Conservation Area. Five acres of well established grounds with old trees and delightful herbaceous borders sweep down to meadows bordering the Waveney River, marking the county boundary.

Guests enjoy homemade cakes on arrival. Other meals include seasonal vegetables and honey from the garden when available. This family home makes a superb bed and breakfast base for anyone wanting to spend time in East Anglia, a lovely part of England which is steeped in history.

The house has been elegantly restored, with antique furniture, interesting paintings and restful colour schemes. In winter guests enjoy log fires in the drawing room and dining room. There are two guest bedrooms, both south facing with river views, a super king (that can also be arranged as a twin) with an en suite bathroom and a king size with private bathroom. Fine linens, flat screen televisions and sumptuous towels and toiletries are provided.

The Hosts

Laurence and Susie have owned The Old Rectory since the late 1990's having moved their family from London where they enjoyed careers in property. As well as being on hand for their guests, they are involved with a specialised property investment and management business and have two teenage sons. Laurence and Susie enjoy cooking and would be delighted to prepare dinner by prior arrangement. They both love entertaining, outdoor pursuits and gardening and will be happy to share their local knowledge.

The Location

The market towns of Bungay and Beccles are nearby and the Waveney Valley is a superb base for exploring the Norfolk Broads and East Anglia's rich history. The Cathedral City of Norwich and the Suffolk Heritage Coast are within easy reach, as are various open gardens and National Trust properties.

Laurence & Susie Carr
The Old Rectory
Geldeston Road, Ellingham
Bungay, Suffolk NR35 2ER
Tel: 01508 518462
sec.wolsey@gmail.com
www.oldrectory-waveney.co.uk 3959

Finding Us

Approaching from Bungay along A143, after approx. 2 miles take right turn signed Ellingham Mill. This is Church Road. Pass Ellingham primary school on right. Continue over disused railway bridge, St Mary's Church is ahead. Follow road to left, almost immediately on right is a long hedge with entrance in the middle leading down a gravel drive to The Old Rectory.

Rooms (per person per night incl. breakfast)

1 Super King (6')/Twin Room (en suite)	£55
1 King Size (5') Room (Private)	£45
Weekday Single Supplement	£15
Weekend Single Occupancy	£90-£110

Meals

Dinner (3 courses) (By prior arrangement)	£30

Opening Times

Closed 10th December to 8th January

Payment Options

Facilities & Services

Mark Felton
Flindor Cottage
The Street
Framsden
Suffolk IP14 6HG
Tel: 01473 890058
mark@flindor.com
www.flindorcottage.co.uk   3969

Finding Us
The Street is in the centre of Framsden, off the B1077, which is off the A1120 tourist route. Flindor Cottage is opposite the village pub, The Dobermann.

Rooms (per person per night incl. breakfast)

1 Super King (6') Room (en suite)		£55
1 King Size (5') Room (en suite)		£55
Single supplement		£35

Meals

Supper (2 courses)	£25
Dinner (3 courses)	£30

Opening Times
Open all year

Payment Options

Facilities & Services

The Property
What makes a B&B truly outstanding and a delight to visit? We believe it is everything that's on offer at the 16th century Flindor Cottage in the rural idyll of Framsden in Suffolk, home to Mark Felton and his two children.

Mark has created a luxurious guest suite from a small barn adjoining the main house, a perfect arrangement which offers bed and breakfast guests secluded privacy, the other guest room is newly refurbished and is in the main house. Both are furnished with country antiques with a keen eye for comfortable and thoughtful touches such as the sleigh bed covered in fine cotton sheets. Absolutely nothing has been missed and your comfort is assured.

In winter, guests will appreciate the cosy fires in the main house whilst in the summer the garden has a sheltered terrace to relax on. Tea and scrumptious homemade cakes and biscuits greet guests on arrival and more homemade treats are offered at breakfast and dinner (if you decide to eat in). Altogether Flindor Cottage is simply a delight and we know you will enjoy staying here.

The Hosts
Given the opportunity of a complete change to his life Mark jumped at the chance and enjoys entertaining guests along with his partner, Annabel. Having had a 25 year City career, Mark started a charter fishing business out of Southwold Harbour. Fresh fish is almost always on the menu.

The Location
In the heart of the Suffolk countryside with miles of public footpaths, Flindor Cottage offers a restful country getaway. It is however located just off the A1120 tourist route and is surrounded by numerous tourist attractions. The market towns of Framlingham and Woodbridge are close by and the coastal towns of Aldeburgh and Southwold only a 30 minute drive away. Norwich, Bury St Edmunds and Ipswich can be reached in under 40 minutes.

The Property
Sweep down the long drive to the mellow, 17th century listed Grade II manor house where a warm welcome awaits you. Here, elegant reception rooms filled with lovely antiques, pictures and flowers, create a relaxing country retreat. Individually decorated bedrooms with fine linen add to the serene atmosphere.

Old Whyly is a place for all seasons. In the spring, the garden comes to life with rhododendrons, azaleas, daffodils and tulips creating a blaze of colour. You can play tennis on the hard court or laze by the secluded swimming pool.

The lily scented terrace, with its rose covered pergola, is well used on sunny days and warm summer evenings, as is the drawing room with the blazing fire in winter. You can also enjoy lovely walks through the adjoining private estate at any time of year.

The Hosts
One of the highlights of staying at Old Whyly is the dining experience. Having studied cooking and flower arranging in Paris and London, Sarah is a passionate cook. She enjoys using home grown produce wherever possible, with eggs laid by her prize winning hens and ducks, and honey from the bees in the orchard.

The Location
Old Whyly is the perfect place to stay for the Glyndebourne opera festival, being less than 10 minutes away. There are many historic houses, castles and villages to visit within easy reach. The medieval county town of Lewes with its art and antique shops is close by, as is Brighton, with its famous Pavilion and seaside atmosphere.

Mrs Sarah Burgoyne
Old Whyly
East Hoathly
Sussex BN8 6EL
Tel: 01825 840216
stay@oldwhyly.co.uk
www.oldwhyly.co.uk   1597

Finding Us
A22 3 miles south of Uckfield continue for further 0.5 mile past Halland then take first left off large Shaw roundabout towards East Hoathly, for 0.5 mile, drive on left with post box. Where drive divides into 3 take the central gravel drive to Old Whyly.

Rooms (per person per night incl. breakfast)

3 Super King (6')/Twin Rooms (2 en suite/1 private)	**£47.50-£70**
1 King Size (5') Room (private)	**£47.50-£70**
Single Supplement	**£35**

A small supplement may apply for a one night stay during Glyndebourne Season

Meals
Dinner	**£35**

Opening Times
Closed occasionally

Payment Options

Facilities & Services

Rob & Candida Machin
Prawles Court
Shoreham Lane, Ewhurst Green
Robertsbridge, East Sussex TN32 5RG
Tel: 01580 830136 or 07769 708050
　　　or 07799 576187
info@prawlescourt.com
www.prawlescourt.com　　　　　**1576**

Finding Us

From A21 turn left on to A229 to
Hawkhurst/Maidstone. After 0.1 mile first
right into Merriment Lane. At junction turn
right onto B2244. After 1.2 miles turn left
for Bodiam & Ewhurst Green. Over steam
railway line, 2nd left into Shoreham Lane.
Prawles is signed 0.1 mile on right. Follow
drive to top.

Rooms　(per person per night incl. breakfast)

1 Super King (6') Room　(en suite)　**£75**
3 Super King (6')/Twin Rooms　**£70-£85**
(en suite)
Single Supplement　　　　　　**£40**

Meals

Breakfast only

Opening Times

Closed Christmas, New Year and some
winter months

Payment Options

Facilities & Services

The Property

The promise of 'providing every comfort a guest could
expect' is wonderfully fulfilled with a stay at Prawles Court.
Your hosts Rob and Candida Machin have created an
outstandingly elegant and comfortable home surrounded
by 27 acres of gardens and grounds, ideally located on the
Kent and Sussex border.

Elizabethan in origin, Prawles was later extended in the
Arts and Crafts style by Nathaniel Lloyd and his admiration
for Lutyens' designs is highlighted in the airy rooms and
decorative brickwork and windows. Inglenook fireplaces
in the beamed drawing room and dining room create an
intimate atmosphere to relax in, whilst on warm days the
Orangery and gardens are the perfect places to enjoy
breakfast or afternoon tea.

The bedrooms are simply sublime! Spaciously laid out,
with beautiful furnishings, each is individually designed to
offer complete and utter comfort. Homemade biscuits and
treats are waiting and fine toiletries ensure you can pamper
yourself a little too. Home grown and locally sourced
produce characterises breakfast and there is an excellent
choice of dining venues close by.

The Hosts

Building a home at Prawles Court with Candida and their
three children, Rob enjoys painting, photography, fine wine,
antiques and golf whilst Candida combines her family
with her curtain business. Looking after their menagerie of
animals, home and garden is enjoyed together.

The Location

Prawles Court is within easy reach of Bodiam Castle,
Sissinghurst, Batemans, Scotney Castle, Great Dixter, the
towns of Battle and its surrounding 1066 country, Rye,
Tenterden and Tunbridge Wells. Coastal walks are 20
minutes drive to the south and walkers can access footpaths
from the garden.

The Property

Originally the home of the local apothecary, this delightful Grade II listed Georgian house has been lovingly and sympathetically restored. With wonderful views across the High Weald or Pevensey marshes towards the sea, it sits in beautiful gardens of over two acres, with woodland, a magnificent walled garden bursting with colourful flowers and an avenue of lime trees.

Inside this superb country house, a clever, stylish mix of antiques and classically modern furniture, coupled with lovely colour schemes and soft furnishings creates a welcoming and relaxing ambience. The 'Snug' is perfect to read, relax or even play the piano! The spacious guest rooms have ultra comfortable beds and luxurious en suite bathrooms. All the little extras are on hand to enable guests to unwind entirely.

The delicious breakfasts using locally sourced ingredients are served in the elegant dining room and will set guests up for the day.

The Hosts

Although relatively new to their business, Sara and Simon are already receiving rave reviews. They love entertaining and nothing is too much trouble, including making reservations for guests at local pubs and restaurants. Simon is a business consultant and Sara left her career in higher education to run Boreham House, once the restoration was complete.

Both are well travelled with Sara having lived in the Middle East and Africa. They are very involved in village life and spend many happy hours walking their Norfolk Terrier Rosie, enjoying the glorious countryside surrounding their home.

The Location

Ideally situated for discovering East Sussex and Kent with wonderful walks (the 1066 path is adjacent), beaches, gardens, National Trust properties, 1066 landmarks, castles, museums and other places of interest abound in this area. Visitors to Glyndebourne or the many other festivals and shows taking place each summer will find Boreham House the perfect base.

Simon & Sara Parker
Boreham House, Boreham Hill,
Boreham Street, East Sussex BN27 4SF
Tel: 01323 833719 or 07809 383482
enquiries@borehamhouse.com
www.borehamhouse.com   1573

Finding Us
From East approach Boreham Street on A271 up a hill. As road levels off and see Boreham Street & 30mph sign, Boreham House is 200 metres further on right hand side - look out for distinctive Yew hedge - entrance to courtyard for parking is just after the hedge. Note: if you reach the Bulls Head pub, you have gone about 100 metres too far! From West, on reaching Boreham Street on A271 drive through village past Bulls Head pub on right. Boreham House is 100 metres further on left hand side. Entrance to courtyard for parking is just before the Yew hedge.

Rooms   (per person per night incl. breakfast)

1 Super King (6') Woolner Suite/ Family Suite (en suite)	**£55-£85**
1 Super King (6')/Twin Ashburnham Room (en suite)	**£45-£70**
1 Double (4'6") Kingswell Room (en suite)	**£40-£60**
Single occupancy - 20% less than total room rate.	

Meals
Breakfast only

Opening Times
Closed Christmas

Payment Options

Facilities & Services

The Property

Strand House, in Winchelsea, East Sussex was built in 1425. This listed building might be nearly 600 years old and pre-date Cardinal Wolsey himself but now offers every modern comfort. When built, it was on Winchelsea Harbour, but centuries of silting up means Winchelsea Beach is now in distant view. Set in glorious gardens overlooking adjoining meadows, complete with beehives and grazing sheep, there are areas to relax in and paths to explore – one taking you into town via a medieval Strand Gate in the town walls.

The interior is as interesting and inviting as the exterior. Beams, nooks and crannies, uneven floors and ancient doorways lead you through this lovingly restored home, furnished in a Flemish style with complementing antiques. An honesty bar and a choice of sitting rooms, one with a wood burning stove, are available.

Breakfast is served at separate tables in the dining room, complete with inglenook. Enjoy a full Sussex breakfast, followed by freshly baked croissants and breads, served with locally made preserves or honey from Hugh's beehives.

Luxurious guest bedrooms – one with a four poster bed – are individually furnished and vary in size (as befitting such an historic property) and include towelling robes and hospitality tray with homemade biscuits.

The Hosts

Nothing is too much trouble for Hugh and Mary. Both have many years experience in catering and Mary has had a life-long interest in cooking. Special dietary needs are catered for with ease plus packed lunches and delicious dinners are available by prior arrangement.

The Location

Castles, battlefields, beaches, gardens and stately homes abound and ancient Winchelsea itself is a hidden delight. Located between the High Weald and the Romney Marsh, 2 miles from the famous medieval town of Rye, 7 miles from Hastings and close to the sea. East Sussex has something to interest everyone.

Mary Sullivan & Hugh Davie
Strand House, Tanyards Lane
Winchelsea, East Sussex TN36 4JT
Tel: 01797 226276 or 07889 177120
info@thestrandhouse.co.uk
www.thestrandhouse.co.uk   1572

Finding Us

From London take M2 to Ashford J1 then turn off A2 J7 for Brenzett. At Brenzett go straight across roundabout and follow through Rye. 2 miles beyond Rye, reach Winchelsea. Strand House is on left at bottom of Strand Hill.

Rooms (per person per night incl. breakfast)

1 Super King (6') /Twin Room (en suite)	**£45-£95**
7 King Size (5') Rooms (en suite)	**£45-£95**
1 King Size (5') Room (private)	**£45-£75**
1 Double (4'6") Four Poster Room (en suite)	**£45-£95**

Meals

Supper (2 courses)	**£20**
Dinner (3 courses)	**£34.50**

(On Friday & Saturdays only by arrangement)

Opening Times

Closed Christmas & New Year

Payment Options

Facilities & Services

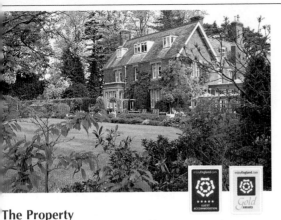

The Property
Fragrances of lavender, honeysuckle, jasmine and roses tumbling over golden stone walls and an air of calm greet guests as they approach Uplands along a drive lined with ancient lime trees.

Inviting and peaceful, guests can wind down in lovingly furnished surroundings. Relax in the spacious drawing room; linger over splendid four course dinners or a lighter supper accompanied with wonderful wines in the candlelit dining room, or in summer, dine al fresco on the terrace.

Choose between the fabulous four poster bedroom with its luxurious en suite bathroom or the Chinese room which can be a double or twin, both of which enjoy a lovely view across the parkland, or the smaller but charming double room overlooking the Orangery and Rose Garden. Whichever room you choose, be spoilt with fresh flowers, crisp bed linen, lovely bathroom accessories and be assured of a scrumptious breakfast when you wake.

The Hosts
Poppy and Graham love chatting over a glass of wine or dinner. Poppy is a picture restorer and art historian. Graham is retired from teaching engineering at Kings College. Both have been Olympic fencers, are recent world champions and enthusiastically compete as veterans. Poppy's creative cooking using fresh local or garden produce, has won many accolades and she thoroughly enjoys spoiling guests. Graham's amazing practical skills keep everything flowing nicely.

The Location
Guests can walk to see the treasures of Upton House. The National Herb Centre is close by, as is Edgehill, site of the first battle of the English Civil War. The gardens of Kiftsgate, Hidcote, Sezincote and Coughton Court are a short drive away, and Charlecote Park, Compton Verney, Warwick Castle, Blenheim Palace, Stratford on Avon and Stow on the Wold and many other Cotswold towns and villages are easily accessible.

Poppy Cooksey and Graham Paul
Uplands House, Upton, Banbury,
Warwickshire OX15 6HJ
Tel: 01295 678663 or 07836 535538
poppy@cotswolds-uplands.co.uk
www.cotswolds-uplands.co.uk   4996

Finding Us
From M40 south, at J11, follow signs to Banbury A422, continue on A422 through Wroxton. After 3.6 miles there is a sign "Upton House 200 yds", in 10 yds turn right into drive marked Uplands Farm. Uplands is first house on right. From M40 north, take J12. Follow signs to Gaydon, turn left in village and follow signs to Upton House. Follow A422, past Upton House and turn left into drive marked Uplands Farm, 30yds after junction signposted to Edgehill & Ratley. Uplands is first house on right.

Rooms (per person per night incl. breakfast)
1 King Size (5') Room (en suite)	£50
1 Super King (6')/Twin Room (en suite)	£60
1 Super King (6') Feature Room (en suite)	£90
Single Supplement	£20

Meals
Supper	£20
Dinner	£35

Opening Times
Closed Christmas and Easter

Payment Options

Facilities & Services

Lucy & John Horner
Austons Down
Saddlebow Lane
Claverdon
Warwickshire
CV35 8PQ
Tel: 01926 842068
mail@austonsdown.com
www.austonsdown.com   5945

Finding Us

Detailed directions available at time of booking.

Rooms (per person per night incl. breakfast)

1 Feature Super King (6') Room (en suite)	£60-£80
1 Super King (6')/Twin Room (en suite)	£55-£80
1 King Size (5') Room (en suite)	£50-£70
Single Supplement	£20

Meals

Supper	from £25
Dinner	from £50

Opening Times

Closed Christmas, New Year & Easter

Payment Options

Facilities & Services

The Property

Set mid way between historic Warwick and Stratford-upon-Avon, in the Vale of Arden, sits a pretty modern Queen Anne style house that offers travellers a tranquil base for exploring this beautiful part of Warwickshire. Austons Down, home to Lucy and John Horner, is surrounded by 100 acres of gardens and grounds where friendly sheep and the family's horses graze together.

A welcoming afternoon tea is served on your arrival as you start to unwind and relax in the informal and comfortable surroundings of this family home. Many of the rooms have the advantage of overlooking the glorious gardens which extend around the house and the large patio offers some of the best views of the particularly fine roses that bloom here.

Local produce, as well as vegetables and fruit from the garden, feature at both breakfast and dinner, if you choose to eat in. Lucy will provide her guests with a packed lunch if requested.

The Hosts

Lucy and John brought their family up in Austons Down before deciding to open the house to guests. They share a love of horses, classic cars and rare breed sheep.

The Location

Warwickshire and the surrounding counties are rich in visitor attractions to suit everyone. Warwick Castle, Shakespeare's Stratford with its wonderful theatre, Kenilworth Castle, Heritage Motor Museum at Gaydon, Coventry Cathedral plus National Trust properties such as Charlecote House, Upton House, Coughton Court, Baddesley Clinton and Packwood House. Blenheim Palace is within reach as is Bicester Village and golf courses galore.

The Property

Bradford-on-Avon straddles the river on the southern edge of the Cotswold Hills, and Priory Steps, originally a terrace of six weavers cottages, enjoys stunning views over the beautiful historic townscape.

Old leather sofas nestle in the library, perfect for a relaxing pre-dinner drink. The dining room, with crackling log fire on chilly evenings, has a door onto the exquisite terraced garden, filled with fragrant roses, clematis and passion flowers clambering over wonderful old Cotswold stone walls.

This light, spacious home was purchased from the world record breaking aviatrix and motor racer, The Hon Mrs Victor Bruce - the first lady to win the Monte Carlo Rally Coupe Des Dames in 1928 and the first Englishwoman to fly solo around the world. Fascinating memorabilia relating to her exploits are displayed in the house.

Five comfortably furnished bedrooms, including 'Mrs Bruce's' with its own sitting room, have their own bathrooms. Priory Steps is perfect for large groups and house parties.

The Hosts

Carey and Diana have been welcoming Wolsey Lodge guests to their home since 1987. Diana is an expertly trained cook and one of her catering jobs included a cricket season cooking for the committee and VIPs at the Oval! Carey, a keen local historian and former Chair of the Town and District tourist associations, will happily advise on the best places to visit.

The Location

With an ancient Saxon chapel, splendid Norman church, 14th century town bridge with lock-up and Tithe Barn, the town is a living history of architecture. It is also central for visiting Bath, Longleat, Lacock Abbey, Castle Combe, the beautiful gardens at Stourhead, Stonehenge, Avebury, and the beautiful Cotswolds.

Carey and Diana Chapman
Priory Steps
Bradford on Avon
Wiltshire
BA15 1NQ
Tel: 01225 862230
priorysteps@clara.co.uk
www.priorysteps.co.uk   5997

Finding Us

Bradford-on-Avon is on the A363, 8 miles south east of Bath, 2 miles north of Trowbridge. Take the first left, towards Bath, just north of Bradford town bridge. Turn left, signed to Turleigh, by thatched cottage. Priory Steps is 100 yards down on the left.

Rooms (per person per night incl. breakfast)

2 King Size (5') Rooms (en suite)	**£51-£60**
1 Super King (6')/Twin Room (en suite)	**£51-£60**
1 Double (4'6") Room (en suite)	**£51-£60**
1 Twin (2 x 3') Room (en suite)	**£51-£60**
Single Supplement	**£30**

Meals

Dinner	**£30**

Opening Times

Open all year

Payment Options

Facilities & Services

The Property
Situated in a tiny hamlet of just four houses and surrounded by fields, Bullocks Horn Cottage is a delightful 200 year old house offering a peaceful and tranquil haven on the fringe of the Cotswolds.

On arrival you are greeted by Liz and Colin with tea and delicious cakes to help you unwind after your journey. The cottage is spacious and beautifully decorated and furnished with fine antique furniture. The twin room has an en suite bathroom and the super king room has a private shower room. Both have simple decor which highlights the glorious views from the windows of the gardens and fields beyond.

Breakfast and dinner are served in the conservatory or in the cool shade of the garden. Vegetables and herbs are used from the kitchen garden together with locally sourced produce. The garden is spectacular - Liz has created a stunning cottage garden with a collection of special and unusual plants with paths meandering around the garden and seating areas that entice you to sit awhile and take pleasure in your surroundings.

The Hosts
Liz and Colin are a very friendly, interesting couple who thoroughly enjoy entertaining guests in their home. Liz is a Cordon Bleu cook and loves gardening and interiors, whilst Colin is a talented artist with a studio in the garden and samples of his work can be seen around the house. When he is not painting he is a keen golfer and fisherman.

The Location
Only a few miles from the historic town of Malmesbury, Bullocks Horn Cottage is the ideal base for visiting some of the most beautiful houses and gardens in England. Malmesbury Abbey, Abbey House Gardens, Westonbirt Arboretum and Berkeley Castle are all within easy reach.

Colin & Liz Legge
Bullocks Horn Cottage
Charlton
Malmesbury
Wiltshire SN16 9DZ
Tel: 01666 577600
bullockshorn@clara.co.uk
www.bullockshorn.co.uk   5964

Finding Us
A429 from Malmesbury take B4040 to Cricklade through Charlton. Past Horse & Groom Pub – ½ mile further, turn left signed Bullocks Horn – No Through Road – on to end of lane, turn right, first drive on left.

Rooms (per person per night incl. breakfast)
1 Twin (2 x 3') Room (en suite)	**£47.50**
1 Super King (6')/Twin Room (private)	**£47.50**
Single Supplement	**£15**

Meals
Supper (2 courses)	**£25**
Dinner (3 courses)	**£30**

Opening Times
Closed Christmas & New Year

Payment Options

Facilities & Services

The Property

The chance to stay in a beautifully restored watermill is rare, so this is a very special opportunity. The restoration, masterminded by Peter, has been sympathetically carried out using old materials and traditional skills. The mill workings are still in place and there is a large glass window looking out onto the mill race complete with a glass panel in the floor to watch the water plummeting below. Hazeland Mill is built on the side of a steep hill in the hamlet of Bremhill, in a beautiful unspoilt valley.

Spacious bedrooms, with en suite bathrooms, are decorated and furnished with luxurious fabrics and fine furniture. There is also a delightful cottage with sitting room and bathroom just opposite the front door of the main house.

The dining room has a lovely wood burning stove and a comfortable sitting room for guests to use. The eight acre gardens include beautifully tended lawns and flower beds with a large vegetable garden. A large terrace offers an alternative dining area or somewhere to just relax and enjoy the views. Jennie is a fine cook who uses home grown fruit and vegetables and locally sourced meat and fish. Breakfast and dinner are not to be missed.

The Hosts

Peter is a commercial property surveyor and enjoys shooting, stalking and fishing whilst Jennie has a background in retail. They are a most welcoming couple who ensure their guests have a wonderful stay and nothing is too much trouble.

The Location

Hazeland Mill is perfectly located for the historic cities of Bath, Devizes and Marlborough. The magnificent Bowood House is within walking distance and there are open air concerts held at Bowood, Lacock and Westonbirt. Longleat House and Wildlife Park, Badminton and the Cotswold Water Park, Westonbirt Arboretum and Avebury are all easily accessible.

Jennie & Peter Shaw
Hazeland Mill
Bremhill
Calne
Wiltshire SN11 9LJ
Tel: 01249 821998 or 07775 824670
jennie@hazelandmill.co.uk   **5959**

Finding Us

M4 Junction 17, A350 to Chippenham, A4 to Calne. Before reaching Calne take left turn signed Bremhill. Follow lane for 1 mile and take first left turn at Dumb Post Pub. Hazeland Mill is at bottom of hill by river.

Rooms (per person per night incl. breakfast)

1 Super King (6') Room (en suite)	**£55**
1 King Size (5') Room (en suite)	**£55**
1 Double (4'6") Room (en suite)	**£55**
Single Supplement	**£10**

Meals

Supper – 2 Courses	**£20**
Dinner – 4 Courses	**£35**

Opening Times

Closed Christmas & New Year

Payment Options

Facilities & Services

Mrs Sheila Virr
Manor Farm House, Ab Lench,
Evesham, Worcestershire WR11 4UP
Tel: 01386 462226
Fax: 01386 462563
sheilavirr@btinternet.com   **5999**

The Property

Tucked away in the heart of rural England, Manor Farm House, set in its lovely garden, is a joy to behold. The house is about 250 years old, built on to a 300 year old cottage.

The much loved house has a comfortable feel in which guests immediately feel at ease. Two reception rooms and a study with television are available for guests, who are impressed by a magnificent Burmese wall hanging in the drawing room, where tea is served on their arrival. The main room of the cottage has original beams and a 7 foot inglenook fireplace, now a 'den' housing a library and collected treasures including an 8 foot Texan Longhorn, the longest ever recorded!

There are two lovely guest bedrooms; the double with en suite bathroom captures the morning sun and has a wonderful garden view. The twin, with original fireplace, is a few paces from the private bathroom. Dressing gowns are provided.

The beautifully laid out garden is at its best in spring when 500 or so daffodils leap into life. Pheasants and badgers seem to think that Manor Farm House is their home address and inquisitive cows peer over the garden wall.

The Hosts

Sheila, and her three little dogs, enjoy entertaining. She spent many happy years working in the City, then in the U.S.A. and Caribbean in a somewhat different capacity! An avid theatre-goer, she still retains links with the R.S.C. at Stratford.

The Location

This is the English countryside at its best, perfect for visiting the beautiful Cotswolds, Stratford, Worcester, Cheltenham, and Warwick Castle. There is also easy access to the M5.

Finding Us

From Worcester take the A422, turn right to Flyford Flavel, at Radford turn right again, follow signs to Lenches. From Stratford take A422 signed Alcester, then signed Worcester. After Inkberrow turn left and follow signs to Lenches. More detailed directions given by telephone.

Rooms (per person per night incl. breakfast)

1 King Size (5') Room	(en suite)	**£45**
1 Twin (2 x 3') Room	(private)	**£40**
Single Supplement		**£10**

Meals

Supper (excl. Sunday)	**£21**
Dinner (excl. Sunday)	**£30**
(By prior arrangement)	

Opening Times

Closed Christmas & New Year

Payment Options

Facilities & Services

Claire Dawkins & John Miller
The Old Rectory
Cradley
Malvern
Worcestershire WR13 5LQ
Tel: 01886 880109 or 07920 801701
oldrectorycradley@btinternet.com
www.oldrectorycradley.com   5958

Finding Us

Junction 7 from M5. Follow signs to Hereford turn off A4103 signed Cradley (opposite Millbank Garage) through village to Old Rectory soon after village shop and Post Office.

Rooms (per person per night incl. breakfast)

1 Super King (6') Room (en suite)	**£70-£75**
1 Super King (6')/Twin (en suite)	**£70**
1 King Size (5') Room (en suite)	**£70-£75**
2 King Size (5') Rooms (private)	**£65**
1 Family Suite (private)	**POA**
Single Supplement	**£35**

Meals

Supper	**£27.50**
Dinner	**£38.50**

Opening Times

Open all year

Payment Options

Facilities & Services

The Property

This magnificent listed Georgian Rectory, dating from 1790 and located in the centre of the village of Cradley, is a delight. Retaining many original features and decorated and furnished in period style, Claire and her partner John have overseen the careful renovation of the house to create a beautiful home.

The hall, surmounted by a stunning atrium, has a curving staircase leading to the beautifully decorated bedrooms on the first floor and a guest sitting room with television and open fireplace at the top of the house. The hall leads into the drawing room with its restored fireplace, carved and gilded wooden pelmets and floor to ceiling windows overlooking the garden. Also leading off the hall are the formal dining room with its superbly sophisticated décor adorned with Claire's fabulous paintings, the Library with large sash windows and a scratched inscription on one pane (ask Claire or John about the historical Clerical dispute) and a delightful morning room.

Home grown vegetables and local produce feature in Claire's inspired cooking and she is happy to prepare packed lunches for guests to enjoy whilst they are out and about.

The Hosts

Claire is a renowned artist and accomplished cook with a passion for walking, whilst businessman John, also a talented cook, plays tennis, squash and racket ball. They both love entertaining and looking after their guests and in their spare time enjoy sailing and the theatre.

The Location

At the foot of the Malvern Hills – perfect for keen walkers to explore the Elgar Route and the Worcestershire Way. The Victorian spa town of Great Malvern and horse racing or shopping at Worcester or Cheltenham are within easy reach. The Three Counties Showground is close by as is Eastnor Castle and the Malvern Theatre. Worcester, Hereford and Gloucester each host the annual Three Choirs Festival in turn.

Judith & Graham Bullock
Kateshill House
Redhill, Bewdley
Worcestershire DY12 2DR
Tel: 01299 401563
info@kateshillhouse.co.uk
www.kateshillhouse.co.uk   5940

Finding Us

From Kidderminster, over the bridge, take second turning left and Kateshill House is half way up the hill on right with sign at bottom of drive.

Rooms (per person per night incl. breakfast)

1 King Size (5') Four Poster Room (en suite)	£55
3 King Size (5') Rooms (en suite)	£55
1 Super King (6')/Twin Room (en suite)	£55
2 Double (4'6") Rooms (en suite)	£47.50
Single Occupancy	£75

Meals

Supper	£25
Dinner	£35

(Both by prior arrangement.
Minimum number of guests may apply)

Opening Times

Open all year

Payment Options

Facilities & Services

The Property

Set on the edge of town within easy walking distance of historic Bewdley, Kateshill House is a magnificent Georgian manor house. Thoughtfully refurbished by the current owners and now boasts twenty first century comfort whilst retaining lots of its original grandeur. Graceful and elegant reception rooms with views across the surrounding lawns and countryside offer a haven of tranquillity.

Each of the seven spacious guest rooms have been individually tailored with a blend of antique and contemporary furniture and fine linen all selected to offer the ultimate in comfort, so relaxation here is totally assured.

As stunning as Kateshill House is, it is the magnificent Sweet Chestnut tree in the garden which cannot fail to grab the attention of visitors. One of fifty Great British Trees selected to mark the Queen's Golden Jubilee, it has a girth of some 33 feet, is around 500 years old and occupies a stately ¼ acre of garden. Keen gardeners will appreciate the labour of love that has created the abundant flower beds and borders which reflect the utter splendour of this very special old manor house.

Home baking and a fine breakfast selection will complete a most comfortable stay and, with an array of fine eateries close by, we are confident a stay of any length here will be utterly and delightfully memorable.

Your Hosts

Cooking, entertaining and gardening are host Judith's passions and, when time allows, travel too. Fine attention to detail means that guests' every need is carefully considered and is one of the many reasons why Kateshill House carries accolades for its excellence.

The Location

Within easy reach of Birmingham, Stratford-upon-Avon, Warwick, Ludlow, Cheltenham, and well situated for visiting Stourport Basin, Tenbury Wells, Arley and Bodenham Arboretums, Kinver Edge and the unusual rock houses, Hartlebury Castle, Harvington Hall, Severn Valley Railway, and West Midlands Safari Park.

Derek & Katrina Gray
The Wold Cottage
Wold Newton
Driffield
East Yorkshire YO25 3HL
Tel: 01262 470696 or 07811 203336
katrina@woldcottage.com
www.woldcottage.com   **8960**

Finding Us

From B1249 turn to Wold Newton, in village turn right by pond, round double bend, first on right, down drive past bungalow.

Rooms (per person per night incl. breakfast)

3 Super King (6') Rooms (en suite)	**£55-£90**
1 Double (4'6") Room (en suite)	**£55-£90**
1 Twin (2 x 3') Room (en suite)	**£55-£90**
1 Family King (5') & Twin (2 x 3') Room (en suite)	**£55-£90**

Meals

Dinner (by prior arrangement)   **£28**

Opening Times

Open all year

Payment Options

Facilities & Services

The Property

Don't be fooled by the name 'The Wold Cottage'. This is a magnificent Grade II listed Georgian Manor House and is country house accommodation at its finest, set in 200 acres of Yorkshire Wolds. Originally a Georgian gentleman's country retreat the house retains many original features and is full of character.

There are four spacious and beautifully decorated bedroom rooms in the main house. In addition there is a nearby converted barn with two further bedrooms, including a family room. All are delightful with crisp Egyptian linen, comfortable chairs and are equipped with televisions, clock-radios and tea making facilities, one has a large four poster bed, and all have wonderful views of the Yorkshire Wolds. The en suite bathrooms are also beautifully finished with lovely bathrobes and toiletries.

This "deliciouslyyorkshire Breakfast Award" winner's meals are sourced using local produce and include vegetables from the garden whenever possible. Complimentary local bottled water, chocolates and biscuits are left in the room. A welcome tea with homemade cake is offered between 4pm and 6pm.

The Hosts

Derek and Katrina are friendly and welcoming hosts who enjoy meeting people and providing guests with an unforgettable stay. They have diversified their working stock and arable farm to welcome guests into their beautiful home.

The Location

Superb location for bird watching, walking along the Yorkshire Wolds Way or the Moors, fishing or golf at Ganton. Visit Castle Howard, Sledmere House or York with it's magnificent Minster and the glorious Yorkshire coast is only 7 miles away so perhaps visit Filey or the famous fishing port of Whitby.

The Property

This secluded Georgian village house with a cream facade is approached through an oak door leading into a well tended garden with half size croquet lawn and large umbrella shaped Yew tree.

Guests arriving late afternoon are welcomed with tea or coffee in the comfortable sitting room, which sets the scene downstairs. The house is furnished with antiques, rugs on polished maple floors, shuttered windows and log fires in winter months.

Elegantly restrained, fully equipped guest rooms overlook the garden, where wild white strawberry plants carpet the rose garden. The larger en suite room features an imposing 17th century Portuguese four poster bed. The second room has an antique French bed and private bathroom. Both bathrooms have large cast iron baths.

The Host

Lesley is an Antiques Dealer. Her small shop is in a converted stable and is full, not only of small antiques but also traditional fisherman's Ganseys, hand knitted to the intricate patterns of the coastal fishing communities, a craft which Lesley has revived.

The Location

Perfectly situated to explore the caves and shores of Flamborough Head, to walk the footpath around the Heritage Coast or visit the RSPB Sanctuary at Bempton, famous for its gannet colony and its puffins in early summer. There are a number of good local pubs within easy walking distance, offering local seafood, when available. Fishing, boat trips and golf are available locally.

Lesley Berry
The Manor House
Flamborough
Bridlington
East Yorkshire YO15 1PD
Tel: 01262 850943 or 07718 415234
gm@flamboroughmanor.co.uk
www.flamboroughmanor.co.uk 8997

Finding Us

From Bridlington take B1255 to Flamborough. Follow Lighthouse signs, past St Oswald's church on right. The Manor House is on next corner (of Lighthouse Road and Tower Street). Look for signs announcing 'Antiques and Sweaters'. For SATNAV use postcode YO15 1PY which leads direct to Lighthouse Road entrance.

Rooms (per person per night incl. breakfast)

1 King Size (5') Room	(private)	**£47**
1 King Size (5') Room	(en suite)	**£52**
Single Supplement		**£15**

Meals
Breakfast only

Opening Times
Closed Christmas

Payment Options

Facilities & Services

The Property

Shallowdale House is the kind of special guest house that, once you have visited, you don't want to share with anyone else because it is so special. This is an outstanding 1960's architect-designed house with huge picture windows to every room, allowing guests to take in spectacular views of the glorious Yorkshire countryside. There is a warm and relaxing atmosphere throughout and a wonderful attention to detail which makes guests return time and time again.

The bedrooms are light, spacious and stylish with all the finishing touches such as television, radio, tea and coffee making equipment, hairdryers and beautiful toiletries, but the best part must surely be waking each morning to the stunning views from the windows.

As if this wasn't enough, Anton and Phillip are the most delightful and attentive hosts one could wish for, with Anton looking after guests and preparing afternoon tea, and Phillip cooking the most exquisite dinners and setting guests up for a days' activities with a hearty breakfast using the finest, and mostly, locally sourced ingredients.

The Hosts

Anton and Phillip have the wonderful ability to make their guests feel they are the most important people in the world. Nothing is too much trouble and they really enjoy providing their guests with an unforgettable experience. They both have a background in art and design which is evident throughout the house and their local knowledge will ensure guests do not miss any of the delights of the area.

The Location

Situated on the southern edge of the North Yorkshire Moors National Park this is a stunning location encompassing moorland, rugged coastline and beautiful countryside with charming villages. Visit Castle Howard, Rievaulx, Byland and Ampleforth Abbeys, Nunnington and Beningbrough Halls, or the historic cities of York and Harrogate which are both close by.

Phillip Gill & Anton van der Horst
Shallowdale House
Ampleforth
York YO62 4DY
Tel: 01439 788325
Fax: 01439 788885
stay@shallowdalehouse.co.uk
www.shallowdalehouse.co.uk   8964

Finding Us

Shallowdale House is situated at the western end of Ampleforth, on the turning to Hambleton. Approach on the 'caravan route' from Thirsk via A19, Coxwold and Wass; or A170 Thirsk to Helmsley, turning right 4 miles after Sutton Bank; or B1363 from York, turning left at Brandsby.

Rooms (per person per night incl. breakfast)

2 Super King (6')/Twin Rooms (en suite)	£70
1 King Size (5'6") Room (private)	£57.50
Single Supplement	£40

Meals

Dinner (4 courses)	£39.50

Opening Times

Closed Christmas, New Year & occasionally

Payment Options

Facilities & Services

The Property

Set behind high garden walls in the pretty North Yorkshire market town of Helmsely sits Ryedale House, an elegant Grade II listed Georgian townhouse offering guests a foothold in a bustling town with an escape to the countryside just moments away.

The house is furnished with a mix of antique and contemporary furniture complemented by sculptures, family photographs and paintings as well as many books for guests to while away their time with, perhaps cosy in the sitting room in the winter or relaxing in the garden on a summer's evening.

Affording excellent views across the town to the castle and garden, the guest bedrooms are located on the first and second floor with private bathrooms for each room. Debbie's flair for interior design is evident in the pretty and highly comfortable décor and guests' every comfort has been provided for including Egyptian cotton bed linen, a well-stocked tea tray, hairdryer, bathrobes and toiletries.

Outside the walled garden is a tranquil refuge that belies its town location and meals served alfresco in the summer are sure to be memorable. Breakfast is a typical North Yorkshire feast of local sausage, bacon and black pudding as well as a selection of homemade jams. Choosing to dine here guarantees equally quality fayre although there are numerous local restaurants to visit also.

The Hosts

Mike was brought up in Castle Howard and is a keen sportsman, representing the UK at the 1984 Winter Olympics for luging, and loves golf, tennis and motor biking. Debbie was a dress designer in London before moving to North Yorkshire in 2000 retaining her love of designing and cooking.

The Location

Situated on the southern edge of Yorkshire Moors National Park, Castle Howard, Ampleforth, Rivaulx and Byland Abbeys, Nunnington, Hovingham, Newby and Beningbrough Halls all close by. York, Harrogate, Scarborough, Whitby and Thirsk are not to be missed.

The Honourable Michael & Debbie Howard
Ryedale House
Bridge Street
Helmsley
North Yorkshire
YO62 5DX
Tel: 01439 771981 or 07767 686383
farleyhoward@msn.com 8947

Finding Us

On entering Helmsley via the road bridge over the river Rye, Ryedale House stands on the east side of Bridge Street.

Rooms (per person per night incl. breakfast)

1 Super King (6') Room (private)	£60-£65
1 King Size (5') Room (private)	£60-£65
Single Supplement	£20

Meals
Dinner	£35

Opening Times
Open all year

Payment Options

Facilities & Services

Janet & Jon Brook
Halsteads Barn
Mewith
Bentham
North Yorkshire LA2 7AR
Tel: 01524 262641
info@halsteadsbarn.co.uk
www.halsteadsbarn.co.uk   8942

Finding Us

Detailed directions are sent with booking confirmation.

Rooms (per person per night incl. breakfast)

1 Super King (6') Room (en suite)	**£57.50**
1 King Size (5') Room (en suite)	**£49**
1 Double (4'6") Room (en suite)	**£46**

Meals

Supper (2 courses)	**£18**
Dinner (4 courses)	**£28**
(both by prior arrangement)	

Opening Times

Closed occasionally

Payment Options

Facilities & Services

The Property

If you want peace and quiet and to get away from it all, look no further than Halsteads Barn. Originally a livestock barn it has been sympathetically extended using a derelict hay barn and lovingly converted into spacious guest accommodation.

A warm welcome, spectacular 360-degree views and fine food await guests. The magnificent vista can also be seen from the super king room. Bedrooms are all en suite with power showers, televisions, DVD players, bathrobes, slippers and most other comforts normally associated with Wolsey Lodges. As well as the lounge, furnished with a stylish mix of antique and contemporary, there is a cosy snug, wood burning stove, reading gallery for guests to enjoy along with an outdoor hot tub with stunning views over the surrounding countryside.

Delicious breakfasts, with eggs from the resident hens, and homemade preserves will set you up for the day. A tasty four course dinner or two course supper cooked on the AGA are available by arrangement, using locally sourced produce. A carefully compiled wine list is available along with a selection of ales, spirits and after dinner drinks.

The Hosts

Janet and Jon Brook are justifiably proud of their achievements and love sharing this beautiful property with their guests, for whom nothing is too much trouble. Originally both in IT, Jon is an acclaimed professional photographer and guests rave about Janet's superb cooking. They share their home with a menagerie of hens, ducks and family pets which all add to the delightful relaxed ambience of this very special sanctuary from the stresses of everyday life.

The Location

On the edge of the Western Dales, Halstead Barns is perfectly placed for visiting the Yorkshire Dales, Southern Lake District and the Forest of Bowland and ideal for walkers, cyclists or just exploring this designated Area of Outstanding Natural Beauty. Ingleton and Settle are within easy range.

Pamela Hudson & James George
Old Wells, Terrington,
York, North Yorkshire YO60 6PP
01653 648029 or 07717 471212
oldwells.uk@gmail.com   **8946**
www.oldwellsbedandbreakfast.co.uk

Finding Us

On A64 northbound from York towards Scarborough take sign towards Castle Howard (approx 10 miles north of York) follow road for 2.5 miles until crossroads marked left to Bulmer. Turn left after half mile, take right signed Ganthorpe & Terrington. Follow road for 3.5.miles through Ganthorpe and down into Terrington. Old Wells is half way up main street on right, opposite the pub.

The Property

Just half an hour from York and within a conservation area that was once a Castle Howard Estate village, Old Wells sits within walled gardens in the centre of Terrington village.

This home offers total luxury and absolute tranquillity. Antiques complement the mellow décor and add to the overall peaceful ambience. The king size bedroom has a luxurious en suite bathroom with bath and power shower. The double bedroom has an en suite bathroom with shower over whilst the twin has an en suite shower room – all three bedrooms have televisions. The fourth double bedroom sits on its own staircase with a private shower room next to it and is quiet and cosy. Delicious breakfasts are enjoyed around the large dining table overlooking the garden, with eggs and preserves sourced from the farm next door and bacon and sausages from an award winning local producer.

Outside, the traditional country garden features abundance of stunning flora and beyond this the family's stable block. By prior arrangement, guests can bring their own horses to enjoy the numerous local trails or perhaps whilst attending a local horse show.

The Hosts

This is the family home to Pamela and her American husband James. Whilst Pamela works as a lawyer in York, James manages IT projects specialising in healthcare. Their time is dedicated to horses and cycling as well as gardening and cooking and, of course, sharing their home with their guests.

The Location

Old Wells at Terrington in North Yorkshire is close to Castle Howard, 20 miles north east of York and near Malton in the Howardian Hills. The North York Moors National Park is on the doorstep and the Yorkshire Dales National Park is near enough for a day out. When dining out, one is spoilt for choice. Pamela and James are happy to assist with table reservations.

Rooms (per person per night incl. breakfast)

1 Super King (6') Room	(en suite)	**£55**
1 King Size (5') Room	(en suite)	**£50**
1 Twin (2 x 3') Room	(en suite)	**£50**
1 Double (4'6") Room	(private)	**£45**
Single Supplement		**£10**

Meals

Supper (2 courses)	**£25**

(Occasionally by prior arrangement)

Opening Times

Open all year

Payment Options

Facilities & Services

The Property

This 17th century listed former farmhouse nestles into the quiet countryside and the surrounding farming community. Warm, welcoming and so hard to leave, it is difficult to believe that an early resident went off to become a general in the American Civil War!

Book-lined walls in the hall, where guests can sit and browse, and an open fire in the sitting room, add to the cosy ambience. Three comfortable bedrooms enjoy lovely views and come with courtesy trays, biscuits, toiletries and fresh flowers for traditional country living. The antique brass double bed is made up with hand-crocheted bed linen and the twin bedroom with its oversize antique white and brass beds has another twin leading off for extra family space. Lie in bed and dream peaceful dreams or wander round the rose-filled garden blooming all summer.

The Hosts

David and Judith's guests experience a real home-from-home. David was a bedding manufacturer so very comfortable beds are assured. Judith is a trained cook, so you can expect great traditional English cooking. She also makes her own bread, jams and marmalades, so breakfast is a rare treat! Judith also concentrates on the garden, tending the vegetables used in her cooking and making sure she has happy hens!

The Location

The Brontë Museum and the houses used as inspiration in the main novels are just 40 minutes away. Museums abound and The Photographic Museum and Eureka (the children's hands-on activity museum) and Mining Museum are easily accessible.

The Huddersfield Choral Society and Leeds Piano Competition are always worth a visit as are the Calderdale and Pennine Way - a haven for walkers.

David and Judith Marriott
Thurst House Farm
Ripponden, Sowerby Bridge,
West Yorkshire HX6 4NN
Tel: 01422 822820
judith@thursthousefarm.co.uk
www.thursthousefarm.co.uk   8983

Finding Us

Ripponden is on the A58, 5 miles east of Junction 22 on M62 and 3 miles west of Sowerby Bridge. At Conservative Club near traffic lights turn up Royd Lane. At top of hill turn right opposite Beehive Inn. Continue straight on for 1 mile. Thurst House Farm is on the right 100 yards past post box. Gateway is beyond blind bend.

Rooms (per person per night incl. breakfast)

1 Double (4'6") Room (en suite)	**£35-£40**
1 Twin (2 x 3'6") Room (en suite)	**£35-£40**
1 Family Twin (2 x 3') Room (en suite)	**£35-£40**
Single Supplement	**£10**

Meals

Dinner	**£25-£27**

Opening Times

Closed Christmas & New Year

Payment Options

Facilities & Services

The Property

Approached via National Trust land in the heart of Brontë country, just outside Hebden Bridge in West Yorkshire and with the Penine Way passing through the grounds, this 19th century historic shooting lodge is the perfect venue for anyone seeking top quality accommodation in luxurious, splendid isolation in magical surroundings and only an hour from Leeds or Manchester.

Recently extensively restored, Walshaw Lodge is beautifully furnished with an elegant melange of fine antiques, family portraits and three grand pianos. On arrival, guests are served tea in one of the elegant drawing rooms, in front of an open fire. A children's playroom is available for younger guests.

Comfortably furnished bedrooms, all with spectacular views, are reached by one of three staircases, and named after landmarks on the moors. All have en suite or private bath/shower rooms and hospitality trays. Delicious breakfasts and, by prior arrangement, dinners are served in the magnificent dining room - which comfortably seats up to 20 - with views over the valley.

The Host

Owned by the Savile family for many generations, Walshaw Lodge is the family home of Canadian born Margaret, a busy professional pianist and a warm, ebullient host. Her sons having fled the nest, she loves entertaining and walking Pickle, her friendly Cavapoo. Margaret will stage a recital before dinner, by arrangement, something very popular with groups, many of whom regularly base themselves at Walshaw Lodge for walking holidays.

The Location

Perfect for rest and relaxation, this brooding landscape was the inspiration for 'Wuthering Heights'. Hebden Bridge - 'the funkiest place to live in Europe'- offers specialist shops, restaurants, bars, pubs and clubs. Pennine Yorkshire is vibrant, contemporary, exciting; history and innovation march hand in hand. Find prehistoric rock art in the morning and Hockney in the afternoon or just walk, climb, cycle or paint.

The Hon Mrs M A Lumley-Savile
Walshaw Lodge
Hebden Bridge, West Yorkshire HX7 7AX
Tel: 01422 842275 & 01422 843937
margaret@lumley-savile.com
www.walshawlodge.com   8936

Finding Us

Satnav with postcode HX7 7AX takes you to back door. Or from Hebden Bridge take road up hill towards Keighley. Turn half left up hill past houses on left. Signed Hardcastle Crags/ Midgehole (no through road). Follow road until end when you come to a National Trust gate (car park on right). Go through the gate and straight up hill through trees (about 3 miles). Half way to house you pass Gibson Mill, oldest mill in Yorkshire.

Rooms   (per person per night incl. breakfast)

4 Super King (6')/ Twin Rooms (private)	£60-£75
1 Super King (6')/ Twin Suite (en suite)	£70-£85
1 Super King (6')/Twin Room (en suite)	£60-£75
2 Single (4'6") Rooms (private)	£60
Single Supplement	£25

Meals

Dinner (3 courses) (By prior arrangement)	£35

Opening Times

Open all year

Payment Options

Facilities & Services

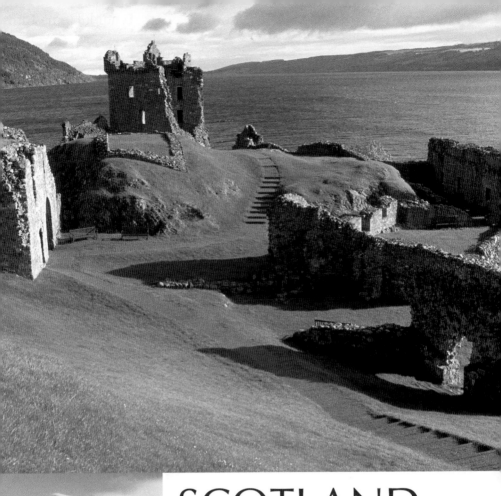

SCOTLAND AWAITS YOU

Scotland is a truly distinct land. From the snow-capped highlands to the balmy Western shores and to the sophisticated atmosphere of its famous cities and the countryside steeped in history and wildlife, it is a land like no other.

Whatever you have planned - walking, sightseeing, cycling or shopping, you're sure to appreciate returning to your tranquil and welcoming Wolsey Lodge where the promise of good company and dinner, either with your hosts or close-by, will invigorate you for the next day.

From top: Loch Ness; Morar, Scottish Highlands; Glamis Castle, Tayside.

The Property

Unwind in a haven of tranquillity just a 20 minute drive from Aberdeen airport. This listed farmhouse, built by hostess Veronica's McCombie ancestors in 1762, nestles in its own 300 acres of land where cattle, sheep and horses feed and roe deer wander.

Inside, through the impressive galleried entrance hall, you will find the gracious drawing room, furnished with family antiques and portraits, with a roaring log fire in colder weather. Delicious candlelit dinners and massive breakfasts are served in the tranquil dining room, twinkling with Georgian family silver and glass.

In the morning, you will wake to the sound of the birds and the sight of the deer from your comfortable en suite bedroom with spectacular far reaching hill views in two directions.

The Hosts

Veronica and John are an informal and friendly couple whose outgoing manner immediately helps guests to feel at home. Veronica, a Cordon Bleu cook, is enjoying entertaining extensively again now that her three children are grown up and her horses have become pensioners. John is a Chartered Surveyor who enjoys all sport and country pursuits.

The Location

Lynturk is at the heart of Aberdeenshire with both private and National Trust castles and magnificent gardens close by in every direction. The local village of Alford is home to the Grampian Transport Museum, a heritage centre and a country park with its own miniature railway. Aberdeen is close by, as is the fascinating northern coastline with its pretty fishing villages. Westward, you'll find Speyside and the whisky distilleries and Royal Deeside is 15 minutes away to the south.

John & Veronica Evans-Freke
Lynturk Home Farm
Tough, by Alford
Aberdeenshire AB33 8HU
Tel: 01975 562504
lynturk@hotmail.com   **9970**

Finding Us

From Aberdeen take A944 towards Alford. Turn left 1 mile before Whitehouse, signed Tough and Muir of Fowlis. Stay on this road for 2 miles. Lynturk is signed on left.

Rooms (per person per night incl. breakfast)

1 King Size (5') Room	(en suite)	**£50**
1 Super King (6') /Twin Room (en suite)		**£50**
1 Emperor (7')/Twin Room (en suite)		**£50**
Single Occupancy		**£60**

Meals

Dinner	**£30**

Opening Times

Closed occasionally

Payment Options

Facilities & Services

Stephen & Rose Rickman
Newtonmill House
By Brechin
Angus DD9 7PZ
Tel: 01356 622533 or 07793169482
rrickman@srickman.co.uk
www.newtonmillhouse.co.uk   9937

Finding Us

From the Aberdeen/Dundee A90 trunk road take B966 towards Edzell. Newtonmill House front drive entrance is one mile from the turning off the A90 on the left. The front drive entrance is distinguished by stone pillars and a gate lodge.

The Property

Approach Newtonmill House, situated between Brechin and Edzell in the beautiful county of Angus and drive through the pillared entrance to take a step back in time. This Grade B listed 18th century laird's house is one of the most beautiful in Scotland. Set in its own rural estate, guests will delight in its famed traditional walled garden that brims with herbaceous, and spring and autumn gardens. Meals include fruit and vegetables grown in the garden and fresh eggs from Rose's hens.

One cannot help feeling at home here with rooms marked with endearing personal touches and decorated with pretty wall coverings and fabrics. A traditional Wolsey Lodges welcome and tea marks your arrival and whilst you sample these delights you will start to appreciate how special this beautiful house is.

The rooms, furnished with painted antique furniture, are delightful - the twin room with en suite bathroom gazes down over the walled garden and the double room with private bathroom looks out over a rose filled courtyard. Character and history abound in this house which had connections with Glamis Castle - The Queen Mother was a frequent visitor and donated plants to the garden.

The Hosts

Stephen and Rose have lived at Newtonmill House for over 30 years. Rose is a Cordon Bleu cook and enjoys creating dishes using fresh local produce. Stephen runs the family business from home and is a keen sailor. They go out of their way to make guests feel welcome - weather forecasts are provided at breakfast time for those guests involved in outdoor activities!

The Location

Access from the main Aberdeen to Dundee road makes this an ideal stopover from Edinburgh, Glasgow, Dundee and Aberdeen as well as a great destination in itself. Places of interest are only a short distance away. An ideal location for accessing the Cairngorm National Park with its Angus Glens and the coastline from Kincardineshire to Fife.

Rooms (per person per night incl. breakfast)

1 King Size (5') Room	(private)	£50
1 Twin (2 x 3') Room	(en suite)	£55
Single Supplement		£15

Meals

Supper	£28
Dinner	£36
Packed Lunch	£10

Opening Times
Closed Christmas

Payment Options

Facilities & Services

Maria & Roger Soep
Roineabhal
Kilchrenan
Taynuilt
Argyll
PA35 1HD
Tel: 01866 833207
maria@roineabhal.com
www.roineabhal.com   9909

Finding Us
Detailed directions available on request.

Rooms (per person per night incl. breakfast)

2 Double (4'6") Rooms (en suite)	£55
1 Twin (2 x 3') Room (en suite)	£55
Single Supplement	£25

Meals

Supper Platter	£25

Opening Times
Closed November to Easter

Payment Options

Facilities & Services

The Property

Roineabhal is a luxurious retreat set in the magical Glens of West Argyll where you are assured of a warm welcome. With wonderful lawns sloping to the babbling burn and a productive vegetable garden, this wood and stone house was recently built by the owner himself and offers every modern comfort.

The three guest rooms all have scenic views. The ground floor bedroom has been adapted for the less mobile guest. Upstairs, the bedrooms both have en suite shower rooms and have each been lovingly furnished with pieces collected and restored by the Soeps over the years. Television, hairdryer, hospitality tray and home-made shortbread add an extra touch of comfort.

The breakfasts are a real feast to set guests up for the day and in true Scottish style, porridge and kippers feature on the menu as well as a full Scottish breakfast complete with black pudding.

The Hosts

The Soeps are ideal hosts – Maria's family background is in hotels, assisting her parents from her teens and then travelling the world prior to settling back in Argyll. Roger's background is in marine engineering and he now runs an office machinery business servicing Argyll and beyond. They are very active and enjoy walking their dog McDuff across the glorious local hills.

They are happy to recommend local restaurants or arrange a local and home grown platter with sweet for supper, and love sharing their knowledge of the surrounding area.

The Location

Loch Awe is one of the largest freshwater lochs in Argyll & Bute, ideal for leisure activities, particularly walking and fishing, and Roineabhal is perfectly situated for day trips to Glencoe, Inveraray, Oban and the Isles.

The Property

This spacious, archetypally Victorian, Scottish country house in Port Appin overlooking the banks of Loch Linnhe and the Sound of Shuna is ideal for exploring this beautiful area of Argyll. Keen horticulturists will love it here, with its ten acres of lovingly tended gardens where guests can enjoy weeping elms, ponds and an abundance of rhododendrons.

Three generously proportioned and comfortable bedrooms (one with four poster), each en suite, are individually furnished with antiques. All modern comforts are provided for including Wi-Fi, television and tea/coffee making facilities.

Tea and homemade cake is provided on arrival. Meals are taken en famille in the elegant dining room which is furnished, as the rest of the house, with a stylish collection of interesting antiques, porcelain, paintings and fine furnishings.

The Hosts

Justifiably proud of her family's restoration of the garden, which has taken some 25 years, Janet really enjoys sharing her home with guests. When she isn't gardening, she is busy baking, preparing delicious home-cooked breakfasts and, by prior arrangement, dinners. She uses produce from her own kitchen garden and locally sourced fresh seafood and meat. Janet can arrange clay pigeon shooting, golf and fishing.

The Location

Situated just 20 miles north of Oban, the main ferry port in Argyll for the Western Isles, perfect for touring the beautiful West Coast of Scotland. The great outdoors certainly beckons here, cycling, mountaineering, fishing, shooting, wildlife watching, sailing and other water sports are on hand, as well as the Scottish Sealife Centre.

Mrs Janet Glaisher
Druimneil House
Port Appin
Argyll PA38 4DQ
Tel: 01631 730228
druimneilhouse@btinternet.com
www.appinaccommodation.co.uk 9904

Finding Us
Detailed directions on request.

Rooms (per person per night incl. breakfast)

1 Double (4'6") Four Poster Room (en suite)	**£55**
2 Twin (2 x 3') Rooms (en suite)	**£55**

Meals

Dinner (3 courses) (By prior arrangement)	**£26**

Opening Times
Open all year

Payment Options

Facilities & Services

The Property

The delicious meals served to guests at Cosses Country House are reason alone to visit this fabulous foodie paradise in this beautiful area of South West Scotland!

Set in twelve acres of woodland and garden, in a hidden valley, this little piece of heaven is a wonderful retreat to unwind from the stresses of today's living.

Black labrador, Monty will escort you on a magical walk with views out to sea towards Ireland, Ailsa Craig, the Mull of Kintyre and Arran. Enjoy afternoon tea in a secluded garden, by Chailoch Burn, a glass of wine at the Hide by the pond or drinks in front of a blazing log fire.

Two spacious suites (very private) across the courtyard and the garden room within the main house are classically decorated and cleverly co-ordinated with every last detail in mind.

The Hosts

Robin and Susan love having guests and sharing their passion for superb food and wine. Home grown produce from the kitchen garden, locally reared meat, game, cheese and freshly caught seafood tempt the taste buds. Susan has written a book about the local food, history and all that there is to see and do in the area. Robin is an accountant with a keen interest in sport, whilst Susan tends the garden and walks the dogs when not looking after guests. Friends and guests describe them as 'perfect hosts'.

The Location

Two hours from Glasgow Airport, or 20 minutes from Irish Ferry Terminals, it is an idyllic country setting, close to the sea, to explore South West Scotland. Walking, cycling or motoring through the myriad of quiet roads, visiting the abbeys, castles or standing stones in an area steeped in history, or exploring beautiful gardens, golf or fishing, offers something for everyone.

Robin & Susan Crosthwaite
Cosses Country House
Ballantrae, Ayrshire KA26 0LR
Tel: 01465 831363 or 07436 810013
staying@cossescountryhouse.com
www.cossescountryhouse.com   9996

Finding Us

From north/south take A77 to Ballantrae. From north go through Ballantrae, over the River Stinchar, then first left (Ballantrae Holiday Park sign). Cosses is 2 miles on the right. From south approach village and turn right before 30mph signs as above.

Rooms   (per person per night incl. breakfast)

1 King Size (5') Room (en suite)	**£55**
2 King Size (5')/Twin Suites with sitting rooms (en suite)	**£65**
Single Occupancy	**£85**

Meals

Dinner	**£35-£40**

Opening Times

Closed Christmas, New Year & occasionally

Payment Options

Facilities & Services

The Property

Chipperkyle is a rather unique gem amongst Scottish country houses. It is a wonderful Georgian Grade B listed Laird's House set in rolling farmland, complete with washhouses and stable courtyard at the back. Your hosts, Willie and Catriona, are justifiably proud of their home and go to great lengths to make their guests feel welcome, serving tea and 'something homemade' on arrival.

Inside, the light and airy rooms are beautifully decorated and furnished, all set against a backdrop of magnificent views in all directions. The double bedroom is comfortable and luxurious and has a large en suite bathroom whilst the twin room has its own private bathroom just one step away. Both bedrooms are furnished with gorgeous white bed linen and the bathrooms with soft, fluffy towels.

Outside there is a large garden with lawns, shrubs and mature trees to walk around, a tennis court in the old kitchen garden and the surrounding fields are home to cattle, sheep, donkeys, pet lambs and the hens that provide the eggs for breakfast. With outdoor sitting areas, guests are invited to enjoy the wonderful, big, often starlit skies, listen to the enchanting bird song and to simply sit back and indulge in total relaxation.

The Hosts

Willie and Catriona are a most hospitable and welcoming couple. Catriona pays special attention to every detail to make your stay enjoyable, and Willie has a wealth of knowledge about Scotland and the local area that makes all the difference to making the most of their wonderful location.

The Location

This is a wonderful area for walking and cycling, top class golf courses, fishing on lochs and rivers, wildlife and bird watching. Nearby, Kirkcudbright is a well known artists' town, whilst Wigtown, like Hay-on-Wye, is a great book centre. Catriona will be able to advise you on the best gardens and museums to visit and there are historic castles and houses to discover and beautiful countryside to explore.

Catriona & Willie Dickson
Chipperkyle
Kirkpatrick-Durham
Castle Douglas
Kirkcudbrightshire DG7 3EY
Tel: 01556 650223
wolseylodge@chipperkyle.co.uk
www.chipperkyle.co.uk   9935

Finding Us

From M6/A74 follow signs to Dumfries/ Stranraer. Take ring road round Dumfries taking A75 to Stranraer. After 12 miles at Springholm turn right to Kirkpatrick-Durham 1¼ miles. At KPD crossroads turn left and after 0.8 miles there is a white cottage on right and Chipperkyle is marked on the gate.

Rooms (per person per night incl. breakfast)

1 Super King (6') Room (en suite)	**£55**
1 Twin Room (2 x 3'6") Room (private)	**£55**
Single occupancy	**£75-£90**

Meals

Breakfast only

Opening Times

Closed Christmas

Payment Options

Facilities & Services

The Property

Holmhill Country House is set in seven acres, with magnificent views of the Keir Hills, and is a five minute walk to the village of Thornhill. Built by a Duke of Buccleuch around 1760, it was part of the estate until 2010 when purchased by Stewart and Rosie. They have refurbished it with a charming and stylish mix of antique and contemporary furniture and fabulous soft furnishings.

Guests are offered tea and homemade shortbread in the elegant lounge on arrival. The generously proportioned bedrooms have super king beds and are en suite, two with exceptionally spacious bathrooms, with roll top or slipper bath and the ground floor room with a power shower. Flat screen television, Egyptian cotton bed linen, bathrobes and indulgent toiletries add that extra touch of luxury.

Visitors are welcome to explore the extensive grounds, which are complete with horses and woodland – perfect for family holidays.

The Hosts

Rosie and Stewart moved from Edinburgh. They bought Holmhill to make it their home but the layout of the house affords guests as much peace and privacy as they wish. Rosie originates from the area, and is a former special needs teacher, and Stewart, a consulting actuary. They are both keen participants in the Scottish sport of curling.

Their warm welcome and delicious food is always much appreciated. Homemade preserves and muesli are served at breakfast and produce is sourced locally where possible.

The Location

The Dumfries and Galloway area is steeped in history, wildlife, adventure parks and outdoor pursuits. The beautiful countryside, adjacent to the Southern Upland Way, is perfect for walkers and cyclists, and golf, fishing or shooting can be arranged. There are National Trust for Scotland attractions within easy reach. With local arts and music festivals too, it is the ideal area to relax and explore, yet Glasgow, Edinburgh and Carlisle are only about an hour's drive.

Stewart & Rosie Lee
Holmhill Country House
Holmhill
Thornhill
Dumfries & Galloway
DG3 4AB
Tel: 01848 332239 or 07884 077228
info@holmhill.co.uk
www.holmhill.co.uk   **9911**

Finding Us
Detailed directions available on request.

Rooms (per person per night incl. breakfast)

2 Super King (6')/ Twin Rooms (en suite)	**£55**
1 Super King (6') (en suite)	**£55**
Single Supplement	**£25**
Discounts available for stays of 2 nights or more	

Meals

Supper (2 courses)	from **£23**
Dinner (3 Courses)	from **£30**

Opening Times
Closed Christmas & New Year

Payment Options

Facilities & Services

Bill & Loraine Frew
Byreburnfoot House
Canonbie
Dumfries & Galloway
DG14 0XB
Tel: 01387 371209 or 07764 194901
enquiries@byreburnfoot.co.uk
www.byreburnfoot.co.uk   **9905**

Finding Us
From South, leave M6 at J44, follow A7
North to Scotland. From North leave M74
at J21. Turn right beyond Evertown, cross
A7 into Canonbie, turn left at hotel. From
Canonbie take B6357 signed Newcastleton.
Turn left immediately crossing river bridge
with traffic lights. Continue north for about a
mile, Byreburnfoot House is on right beyond
saw mill, opposite white cottages. Enter by
main gate, park by front door.

The Property
This delightful sandstone Victorian forester's house nestles
on the banks of the salmon-rich Border Esk and is tucked
away down a gravelled drive, set in 1.5 acres of well
stocked gardens. It offers a great base, not only for keen fly
fishers but also for anyone wanting to explore or relax in
the lovely Scottish Borders. The sound of the river provides
soothing background noise and the views from the house
are spectacular.

The interior is stylishly furnished with a mix of contemporary
elegance and interesting antiques and there are three
bedrooms, each with en suite or private facilities. Every
bedroom overlooks the beautiful gardens or the river and is
comfortably furnished with fine linens, luxury toiletries and
all mod cons one would expect in such a fabulous home.
Guests are offered home baked treats on arrival

Hearty breakfasts include home baked bread, eggs from
resident hens and homemade preserves. Delicious dinners
are available for visitors by arrangement, where guests will
reap the benefits of the hosts superb cooking and produce
from their organic vegetable garden, home grown fruit and
locally sourced meat and fish.

The Hosts
Bill and Loraine bought Byeburnfoot House on retirement
in 2006. They completely refurbished it and now love
sharing it with their guests. Splitting duties – Loraine is a keen
gardener and Bill a superb cook – they still have plenty of
time to welcome visitors. Bill is also a keen fisherman and is
happy to arrange fishing for guests.

The Location
Dumfries & Galloway offers much to see and do as well
as being a convenient place to break a long journey north
or south. With great walking and cycling, fishing, golf and
many beautiful gardens, not forgetting museums, farm parks,
activity centres and stately homes, there is something here
for all ages and interests.

Rooms (per person per night incl. breakfast)
2 King Size (5') Rooms (en suite)	**£55**
1 Super King (6')/Twin Room (private)	**£55**
Single Occupancy	**£70**

Meals
Dinner (3 courses) (By prior arrangement)	**£30**

Opening Times
Open all year

Payment Options

Facilities & Services

Andrew Crosbie
Irish Gait
29 Irish Street
Dumfries
Dumfries & Galloway
DG1 2PJ
Tel: 07791 540535
fathercrosbie@btinternet.com
www.irishgait.com   9902

Finding Us

Located on the Dumfries bank of the Nith on a Feu which stretches between Irish Street (DG1 2PJ and the Whitesands (DG1 2RX). By foot use the postcode DG1 2PJ by car use DG1 2RX.

Rooms (per person per night incl. breakfast)

2 Super King (6') Rooms (en suite)	**£40**
1 Twin (2 x 3') Room (en suite)	**£40**

Meals

Supper   **£30**

Opening Times

Open all year

Payment Options

£

Facilities & Services

The Property

Ideally situated in central Dumfries and offering an opportunity to stay in one of its most notable, ancient houses. Irish Gait - this historic town's only surviving merchant's house - dates from the late 1600s and has been host to many famous people including James Boswell, Thomas Carlyle, Robert Burns and Bonnie Prince Charlie. Overlooking the banks of the Nith, rooms have river or parkland views. Original features include some of Scotland's earliest sash and case windows and 17th century panelling.

Arrive via the private car park and ascend the elegant stone double staircase. In front of the house is a delightful, private walled garden, which guests may use. Inside, the house is lovingly restored, furnished in keeping with its heritage, including many interesting paintings but offering contemporary comforts.

Bedrooms have tea/coffee-making facilities, Wi-Fi, top quality linens and wonderfully comfortable beds and en suite bathrooms with shower. There is an elegant sitting room for guests to use. Delicious breakfasts (and suppers, by prior arrangement) are served in the splendid dining room.

The Host

Father Andrew Crosbie is Anglican Priest of St Bride's (Greyfriars Kirk), which owns and runs Irish Gait. Andrew's family is closely connected with Dumfries, giving him detailed knowledge of the area and its history. A very warm and hospitable host, Andrew is also a superb cook and his full Scottish breakfasts, using locally sourced ingredients, are always popular.

The Location

Irish Gait is a short walk from the centre of Dumfries, and its many fascinating attractions, including Burns House, the Robert Burns Centre and Dumfries Museum (with Camera Obscura). The town is the largest in Dumfries & Galloway and an excellent base from which to explore this beautiful and interesting region, home to many arts and music festivals. Outdoor enthusiasts will be spoilt for choice in terms of walks, castles, gardens, nature reserves and much, much more.

Mrs Caroline Scott
The Dean
Dean Road
Longniddry
East Lothian EH32 0PN
Tel: 01875 853272 or 07921 723272
caroline.rede@yahoo.co.uk   **9906**
www.thedeanbandblongniddry.co.uk

Finding Us
Detailed instructions available at time of booking.

Rooms (per person per night incl. breakfast)

2 Super King (6') Rooms (en suite)	**£57.50**
1 Super King (6')/Twin B&B Room (private)	**£45**
Single supplement	**£15**

A minimum 2 night stay applies to the en suite rooms.

Meals

Supper	(2 Courses)	**£17.50**
Dinner	(3 Courses)	**£30**

(Both by prior arrangement)

Opening Times
Open all year

Payment Options

Facilities & Services

The Property
The Dean, a beautiful three storey listed property with distinctive blue and white Dutch-style gables, is a fine example of Scottish Arts & Crafts architecture. Bordering Longniddry Golf Course (which welcomes non members) this outstanding Wolsey Lodge has magnificent views of the Firth of Forth towards the Ochil Hills. Visitors enjoying the large, pretty garden find it amazingly tranquil – the only noise being birdsong and the 'crack' of golf swings!

The house is classically furnished with interesting antiques, glass, furniture and paintings, and has three spacious bedrooms, all with good-sized bathrooms, two being en suite.

Crisp linens, cosy rugs, elegant cushions and top notch toiletries, tea/coffee making facilities and delicious breakfasts all add to a wonderful experience. Guests can relax in front of an open fire or use the tennis court, depending on the weather.

The Host
Caroline's past career as an interior designer is evident in the exceptional décor of The Dean and her other skills include preparing fabulous meals for guests. Dinner is available by prior arrangement, using local produce such as freshly caught fish, and served in the elegant dining room or the cosy, big and comfortable kitchen. Caroline was born locally and is thus well versed in local knowledge, which she is always pleased to share.

The Location
Being 12 miles from Edinburgh, close to the A1 and just 20 minutes from town via the frequent trains makes The Dean ideal for sightseeing, shopping or cultural visits to the numerous local attractions. A golfer's paradise, it's handy for many famous courses including Muirfield. The area is steeped in history, with stately homes such as Gosford and Lennoxlove, a distillery, museums (including the Museum of Flight at Haddington). The local beach is only five minutes away and the sandy beaches of Seacliff and North Berwick are easily accessible.

GOLD

The Property

Nestled at the foot of a secluded rhododendron-lined drive on the outskirts of Haddington in East Lothian is Letham House. Only 16 miles from Edinburgh, this 17th century mansion boasts exceptional accommodation and dining in a magical setting. Each of the individually designed suites enjoys south facing views over ten acres of mature private gardens and grounds, while sumptuous fabrics, roaring fires and beautiful antiques evoke a sense of luxury and indulgence.

Elegant staircases and architectural features restored to their former glory reflect a bygone era and are complemented by wonderful bathrooms.

Letham House is a nurturing retreat, offering privacy and tranquillity in majestic parkland. This secret world can be enjoyed exclusively for private parties wishing to take over the house, or by individuals looking to escape for a night or two.

The Hosts

Chris and Barbara Sharman are committed to providing the ultimate Wolsey Lodge experience – style, warmth, luxury and peace – and they succeed magnificently. Barbara was previously a successful Relocation Agent whilst Chris's primary trade is that of a Saddler, running a bespoke leather manufacturing company. Rosie the black labrador is very much part of the family and in the field at the bottom of the garden you will meet Hanka, their beautiful haflinger horse and their donkey Charlie.

The Location

The small market town of Haddington has many excellent restaurants, pubs and shops and is just a mile away. The famous Muirfield Golf Course is one of 30 surrounding golf courses. There are beautiful beaches, the Lammermuir Hills and the Sea Bird Centre in North Berwick. The fabulous cultural and historic capital city of Edinburgh is a mere 25 minutes away with a host of museums, entertainment and shopping facilities.

Chris & Barbara Sharman
Letham House
Haddington
East Lothian
EH41 3SS
Tel: 01620 820055 or 07974 375775
stay@lethamhouse.com
www.lethamhouse.com   **9921**

Finding Us

From A1, South or North, exit at Oak Tree Junction. Follow B6471 signed Haddington. Turn right immediately after 40mph sign, through large stone pillars and go down the drive. Letham House is located 40 minutes from Edinburgh International Airport.

Rooms (per person per night incl. breakfast)

4 Super King (6')/Twin Rooms (en suite)	**£70-£95**
Single occupancy	from **£95**

Meals

Light Supper	**£20**
Dinner	**£35**
(Both by prior arrangement)	

Opening Times

Open all year

Payment Options

Facilities & Services

Michael & Vivien Scott
Windmill House
Coltbridge Gardens
Edinburgh EH12 6AQ
Tel: 0131 3460024
windmillhouse@talktalk.net   **9957**

Finding Us

Situated 1 mile west of Princes Street. From Murrayfield Avenue turn into Coltbridge Avenue then into Coltbridge Gardens. At the end of Coltbridge Gardens fork left up hill on private drive then fork left through stone gate pillars signed Windmill House.

The Property

With Windmill House sitting quietly on a hill surrounded with wild riverside gardens, sloping gently away to a lush river valley and waterfall, you would be forgiven for thinking that you were in the heart of the countryside, miles from anywhere. But you are actually just a mile, as the crow flies, from the city centre, next door to the National Gallery of Modern Art in Edinburgh.

This surprising, three storey Georgian style house welcomes guests into a pillared entrance hall with a galleried staircase. The elegant yet cosy drawing room and dining room both have open fires and a lovely terrace offers incredible views.

The ultra spacious and inviting guest rooms have deeply comfortable beds promising a blissful night's sleep and easy chairs to relax in. Lovely finishing touches include colour television and video and quality soaps and bath essences together with large fluffy white towels in the luxury en suite with bath and power shower.

The eponymous old stone windmill sits in the two acre garden, which is home to ducks, swans and badgers, who come to be fed every night.

The Hosts

Michael is a builder specialising in Georgian and Victorian restoration as well as new houses and Vivien is an interior designer. They are interesting, charming and gregarious hosts and have created a beautiful home which they enjoy sharing with guests.

The Location

Edinburgh is a cosmopolitan city with a world famous festival, museums, galleries, excellent shopping, many restaurants, bars and cafes literally on the doorstep. Paths lead through the garden to a bridge then onto a riverside walk into the city.

Rooms (per person per night incl. breakfast)

1 King Size (5') Room (en suite)	£75-£87.50
2 Twin (2 x 3') Rooms (en suite)	£75-£87.50
Single Occupancy	£150-£175

(A small supplement may apply during the August festivals)

Meals

Breakfast only

Opening Times

Closed Christmas & New Year

Payment Options

Facilities & Services

Ross & Kathleen Birnie
23 Mayfield Gardens
Edinburgh
EH9 2BX
Tel: 0131 667 5806
info@23mayfield.co.uk
www.23mayfield.co.uk   9912

Finding Us
Detailed directions available on booking.

Rooms (per person per night incl. breakfast)

3 King Size (5') Rooms (en suite)	**£40-£85**
5 Super King (6')/Twin Rooms (en suite)	**£40-£85**
Single Supplement	**from £25**

Meals
Breakfast only

Opening Times
Closed occasionally

Payment Options

Facilities & Services

The Property
A substantial Victorian villa in the heart of Edinburgh, 23 Mayfield Gardens is just one mile from the city centre which is easily accessible on foot or by bus. Many original features such as stained glass windows have been retained and this boutique guest house has been decorated in rich colours, offsetting the beautiful wood panelling, reminiscent of a gentleman's club. Sympathetically restored and sumptuously furnished, there are many extras such as newspapers, books, DVDs and games for guests to enjoy.

The eight bedrooms all have en suite shower rooms, goose down pillows, fine linens and bathrobes, Penhaligon's toiletries, a fridge and hospitality tray. Hand carved solid mahogany furniture – one guest room with Jacobean style four-poster - and top quality accessories abound.

Superb breakfasts with a strong Scottish theme are served by candlelight in winter, further adding atmosphere. Guests using the garden can enjoy the hot tub and bicycles are for hire.

The Hosts
Ross and Kathleen both have extensive hospitality experience including Ross's time on the QEII. This is a real family business, with Ross's parents helping out too. They have a young family and really enjoy welcoming guests and sharing their detailed knowledge of Edinburgh and the surrounding area. Their breakfast menu reflects Ross's passion for top quality produce, locally sourced and beautifully presented. A vegetarian menu is available.

The Location
Edinburgh is famous for the Festival each August and also the Military Tattoo. It is en route to the Highlands but a superb destination in its own right, with museums, art galleries, lively nightlife, great shopping and more. For foodies there are some excellent places to visit such as Leith with its food shops and restaurants and the former Royal Yacht Britannia.

The Property

As you arrive in the entrance hall of Greenhead Farm with its welcoming log fire you get the first hint of the pleasures in store for those fortunate enough to stay here. Your journey's end is met with tea and home baked treats served either on a sunny verandah if the weather is fine or in front of the drawing room's warming fire.

The farmhouse dates from c.1840 with loving attention brought to bear on the more recent additions added by your hosts Maggie and Malcolm. Antique furnishings and family portraits adorn the house and plump sofas will draw you to the sitting room to relax and take in the stunning views whilst the abundance of board games and books will inveigle you to linger. The bedrooms are spacious, light and beautifully decorated; each with its own bathroom generously supplied with fluffy towels and bathrobes and scented bath essences.

Outside, there is a lovingly tended garden with croquet lawn, fruit trees and a vegetable garden, which provides food for the table. All this is set in 590 acres of farm and woodland providing enjoyable walks.

The Hosts

Maggie and Malcolm enjoy welcoming their guests as friends. Maggie is an excellent hostess and is a keen gardener and trained cook who loves to use fresh produce from her garden whenever possible. Malcolm is an historian with a wealth of local and Scottish knowledge which he will happily share with guests.

The Location

Greenhead Farm is ideally situated for visiting Edinburgh, Perth and Stirling - cities steeped in history with castles, monuments, museums, galleries and festivals. The world famous golf courses of St Andrews, Gleneagles and Muirfield are within an hours drive and there are excellent walks in the Lomond Hills.

Malcolm & Maggie Strang-Steel
Greenhead Farm
Leslie
Glenrothes
Fife KY6 3JQ
Tel: 01592 840459 or 07814 094818
Fax: 01592 841056
maggie@greenheadfarm.co.uk   **9936**
www.fife-bed-breakfast-glenrothes.co.uk

Finding Us

Leave M90 at exit 5 signed Glenrothes. Follow signs for RSPB Vane Farm on south side of Loch Leven B9097; turn left B920 to Scotlandwell. A911 to Leslie, 1¼ miles farm road on left signed Greenhead of Arnot.

Rooms (per person per night incl. breakfast)

1 Super King (6')/Twin	(private)	£60
1 Super King (6') Room	(en suite)	£55
1 Single (3') Room	(private)	£50
Single Supplement		£15

Meals

Dinner	£33

Opening Times

Closed Christmas & New Year

Payment Options

Facilities & Services

The Property

The turrets on the entrance tower of this Grade A listed Scottish castle with peacocks gracing sweeping lawns, are magically revealed after a winding drive through woodland.

Completed in 1608, the Moncreiff family have lived here since 1747 and yet their colourful ancestry and the 17th century architectural features do not overpower this lovely family home. Guests use the Great Hall with its enormous log fire and family portraits on the first floor as their own sitting room, reached by a winding stone spiral staircase. The generous size comfortable Georgian bedroom is next door with more stone steps leading down to a newly refurbished private bathroom.

Outside, two historic ruins - a 9th century Celtic graveyard and remnants of a ruined medieval church - and a 150 yard 'moat' and doocot sit in parkland. The one acre kitchen garden is also being restored to provide some seasonal vegetables.

The Hosts

Rhoderick and Alison are dedicated to the Castle, the 260 acre estate and their many welcome guests. Rhoderick is Lieutenant to the Chief of the Moncreiff Clan. He and Alison are collecting family history, re-establishing the Castle Library and have published a local history book.

The Location

Most of Central Scotland's major attractions are less than one hour's drive away as are Glasgow, Stirling, Perth, St. Andrews and Edinburgh with its Festival, Tattoo and Highland Show. Loch Leven Nature Reserve with bird watching and trout fishing is on the doorstep as well as lots of pleasant walks.

Rhoderick & Alison Moncreiff
Tullibole Castle
By Crook of Devon, Kinross,
Perth & Kinross KY13 0QN
Tel: 01577 840236
holiday@tulbol.demon.co.uk
www.tulbol.demon.co.uk   9960

Finding Us

M90 Junction 6 (Kinross), c5 miles west along A977, just before Crook of Devon left along B9097 for one mile, drive on left through two stone pillars set back from road. Nearest airport Edinburgh, most convenient station Inverkeithing.

Rooms (per person per night incl. breakfast)

1 Double (4'6") or Twin (2 x 3') Room (private)	**£55**
Single Supplement	**£10**

Meals

Supper	**£20**
Dinner	**£30**

Opening Times

Closed October - April

Payment Options

Facilities & Services

The Property

Set in a tranquil Borders village, Skirling House is a truly unique haven of rest and relaxation, where guests are spoilt with award winning gourmet food, fine wines and exceptional hospitality.

Whimsical wrought iron work figures herald the unusual character of the house - its historical artistic connections and Arts & Crafts simplicity brought into sharp relief in the drawing room with a 16th century carved Florentine ceiling, ornate fireplace and decorative door surround. Guests enjoy this lovely room, the cosy book lined study, conservatory and elegant dining room, all of which overlook the garden and woodlands, rolling away to the Borders hills.

Exquisite bedrooms and bathrooms are all highly individual. Warm, welcoming and well furnished with a great sense of style, they possess special individual touches to surprise. Outside, the mature three acre garden includes a tennis court and an idiosyncratic summerhouse, with a floor mosaic set in pebbles and bottle tops!

The Hosts

Bob is a magician in the kitchen and Isobel is the perfect hostess. Their success at Skirling is influenced by their travels and a real understanding of what people need when they are away from home. They are both bright, charming, easy to talk to and have a passion for excellence.

The Location

Nearby attractions include the next village, Biggar, with award winning museums, Victorian Puppet Theatre and amazing Hogmanay bonfire celebration; Dawyck Botanic Gardens, the World Heritage Site of New Lanark and Peebles; the Scottish Borders and Edinburgh and Glasgow with their myriad historic sites and shopping opportunities.

Bob & Isobel Hunter
Skirling House,
Skirling, Biggar,
Lanarkshire ML12 6HD
Tel: 01899 860274
Fax: 01899 860255
enquiry@skirlinghouse.com
www.skirlinghouse.com   9983

Finding Us

Skirling is on the A72, approximately 2 miles north east of Biggar. Skirling House is a dark coloured wood clad house on the west side of the village green.

Rooms (per person per night incl. breakfast)

1 Super King (6') Room (en suite) **£50-£90**

2 King Size (5') Rooms (en suite) **£50-£90**

2 Super King (6')/ Twin Rooms   **£50-£80** (en suite)

Meals

Dinner   **£30-£35**

Opening Times

Closed Jan - Feb & 1 week in Nov

Payment Options

Facilities & Services

Veronica Maclean
Westfield House
Elgin
Moray
Morayshire IV30 8XL
Tel: 01343 547308
veronica.maclean@yahoo.co.uk
www.westfieldhouseelgin.co.uk 9907

Finding Us

From Elgin A96 west for Forres and
Inverness, after 2.5 miles, right onto B9013
for Burghead, after 1 mile signed right at
crossroads continue to Westfield House.

The Property

Westfield House is a gorgeous stone-built house offering
traditional Highland hospitality. Just three miles from the
busy town of Elgin, yet surrounded by the Maclean's 500
acres of rich farmland, it has been home to the family for
generations. This historic house dates from the 16th century
and is the epitome of a fine Highland home, even down to
the tartan staircase!

Set in beautiful gardens, complete with tennis court, walled
garden and immaculate flower beds and lawns. Furnishings
include Maclean tartan, fine antiques and family portraits.
Guests have their own spacious sitting room and breakfast is
served in the large, elegant dining room.

The generously proportioned rooms are cosy and well
appointed. Bedrooms have en suite facilities, except the
single, which has an adjacent private bathroom. Top
quality linen, plump pillows, magnificent views and a
fabulous Wolsey Lodge breakfast to wake up to, come as
standard here.

The Host

Veronica is a former Montessori teacher and had her own
playgroup in the house. Now, as well as looking after her
guests, she is very involved in charity work and holds fund
raising events at Westfield House. She will be happy to
recommend several local pubs in the area for eating out in
the evening.

The Location

The area has much to offer including Spynie Palace, Duffus
Castle, Elgin Cathedral and boat trips to observe the Moray
Firth Dolphins. It is within easy driving distance of Inverness
– gateway to Loch Ness - and Culloden battlefield. Wildlife
walks, fishing, shooting, golf, shopping for Scottish crafts are
all readily available and the region is steeped in history and
Highland castles to explore.

Rooms (per person per night incl. breakfast)

2 Twin (2 x 3') Rooms	(en suite)	**£50**
1 Single (4') Room	(private)	**£55**
Single occupancy		**£55**

Meals
Breakfast only

Opening Times
Closed Christmas & New Year

Payment Options

Facilities & Services

The Property

Old Kippenross is a magical architectural gem, quite unique in Scotland, tucked away in a sheltered sunny position in a wooded valley beside the River Allan.

Guests can walk beside the river and in the grounds among rare mature trees and abundant wildlife.

The 'ancient tower' was built in 1448 and was confirmed as a Barony in 1507. In 1633 it was extended to a fortified L-shaped tower house. It has been painted pink ever since the battle of Sheriffmuir in 1715, a sign that it was a safe house for Jacobite supporters.

The ground floor is fascinating with a vaulted ceiling, an arched fireplace and a log fire. A spiral stair leads up to the 'Blue Room', a twin bedded room with an en suite bathroom and a small single room for a child or relation. Up again is the 'Tower Bedroom' with a king size double bed and en suite bathroom. The bedrooms are prettily decorated and face south with views to the river where roe deer can often be seen browsing.

The Hosts

Susan and Patrick will give you a warm welcome. They are delighted to share their home with you and they dine with their guests. Susan has a flair for cooking and the delicious dinners, served in the lovely vaulted dining room, often include wild salmon from their own river, local game and organic fruit and vegetables from the garden. Patrick is a keen ornithologist.

The Location

Stirling Castle, the Wallace Monument, Doune Castle and Dunblane Cathedral are very close, and Old Kippenross is ideally placed for visiting the Trossachs National Park, Castle Campbell, Falkland Palace and Gleneagles. Edinburgh and Glasgow can both be reached in under an hour by car, and Old Kippenross is 3 minutes drive from a railway station which has an excellent service to both cities.

Susan & Patrick Stirling-Aird
Old Kippenross
Dunblane, Perthshire FK15 0LQ
Tel: 01786 824048 or 07837 299718
Fax: 01786 824482
kippenross@hotmail.com   **9994**
**www.aboutscotland.com/stirling/
kippenross.html**

Finding Us

From north and south go to junction 11 on M9/A9 roundabout. At the roundabout take B8033 and after 500 yards turn right over dual carriageway and into entrance by stone gatehouse. Go down drive and immediately after bridge take first fork right along gravelled drive.

Rooms (per person per night incl. breakfast)

1 King Size (5') Room (en suite)	£52-£55
1 Twin (2 x 3')/Super King (6') Room (en suite)	£52-£55
Single Supplement	£15

Meals

Dinner	£30

Opening Times

Open all year

Payment Options

Facilities & Services

John & Tess Monteith
Essendy House
Blairgowrie
Perthshire PH10 6QY
Tel: 01250 884260 or 07841 121538
johnmonteith@hotmail.com
www.essendy.org   9918

Finding Us

Take A93 out of Perth to Blairgowrie
(Glenshee & Braemar). Immediately before
30 mph sign at Blairgowrie, turn left onto
B947. Go past Muirton Nursing Home,
through standing stones, over bridge with
green railings, up hill after bridge and drive
is at the top of the hill on the right - look for
white metal railings.

The Property

Just beyond Perth, at the southern tip of a string of lochs,
sits Essendy House, a B&B bolthole for weary travellers
and a haven for wildlife lovers. Home to Tess and John
Monteith, Essendy House offers quiet comfort, seclusion
and relaxation in abundance and yet close by there is much
to see and do. Dating back to 1715 with more modern
additions, this white-washed country house is surrounded
by rich gardens and farmland beyond.

The guest sitting room offers a relaxing haven at the end of
the day whilst the conservatory leading on to the terrace
is a welcoming retreat on warm days. The bedrooms and
bathrooms are supremely comfortable and attractive with
antique furniture, wonderful linen and toiletries. The views
from the windows are sure to lure you outside where
mature trees, azaleas and rhododendrons are in abundance
and all around are dramatic hill views.

Highland hospitality dictates a generous and hearty
breakfast served in the elegant dining room or on the
terrace to set you up for a day's exploring. Close by there
are castles and lochs, including the renowned Loch of the
Lowes, famous for its Osprey population

Rooms (per person per night incl. breakfast)

1 King Size (5'6") Room	(en suite)	**£55**
1 Twin (2 x 3') Room	(en suite)	**£55**

Meals

Supper	**£25**
(By prior arrangement)	

Opening Times

Closed Christmas & New Year

Payment Options

£ C

Facilities & Services

BYO C ☼ 🐕 🐾 ✔ WiFi 🚭

The Hosts

Tess was a Lloyds broker and is now an artist who is
pleased to offer guidance to guests if they feel like painting
whilst here. John completed a career in the Army and plans
to build boats. They enjoy the mountains of Europe and
have chalets in the Alps where they spend part of the year.

The Location

Between April and September you have the opportunity to
see the Ospreys and on fine days take an energetic hike up
Birnam Hill, famed for its link to Macbeth. Fishing, shooting
and golf are well catered for and the town of Dunkeld boasts
a fine cathedral. Glamis and Blair Atholl Castles are close by
and in winter there is skiing at Glenshee (40 minutes away).

Elizabeth Miles & Mhari Moir
Pool House, Poolewe, Ross-shire IV22 2LD
Tel: 01445 781272
stay@pool-house.co.uk
www.pool-house.co.uk   **9903**

Finding Us

From Inverness follow signs for Ullapool and A835. Carry on until reach Garve village. Take road west (A832) signed Gairloch. Poolewe is 6 miles north of Gairloch and Pool House is situated in centre of village by bridge where river meets the sea. Or take the scenic route from Glasgow via Fort William to Kyle of Lochalsh and take road to Lochcarron and Torridon - slightly longer but classed by the AA as one of top 10 drives in the world!

The Property

Pool House is a spectacular Highland retreat on the shores of Loch Ewe, dating from the 18th century it is steeped in history and has a nautical theme throughout. The location provides stunning views of not only the Loch, but also where the river meets the sea. Lovingly run by two generations of the Harrison family, it is the perfect retreat and has attracted many celebrities.

The large suites, each named after a WWII warship, comprise a large bedroom, en suite bathroom and sitting room. A balcony overlooking the sea and river, a rare glass canopied Edwardian bathing machine, a seven foot four poster bed or a real fire are just a few examples of what is offered.

Superb breakfasts and a set four course dinner (by arrangement) are served in the dining room which is situated only a few feet from the sea and enjoys spectacular views. Most ingredients come from within a 10 mile radius and include hand-dived scallops and crab from Loch Ewe and venison from the local estate.

The Hosts

With 60 years hospitality experience the Harrison parents welcome their guests but have handed the reins to their daughters Elizabeth & Mhairi. Mhairi's husband John is a professional chef and prepares dinner. This notable family can trace its roots back 1000 years and is related to the actor John Wayne and the captain of the ill-fated Titanic.

The Location

Poolewe is located in the centre of Wester Ross. To the north lies Ullapool, the ferry terminal serving Stornoway in the Outer Hebrides and to the south, Kyle of Lochalsh and the Isle of Skye. Five hours drive from Edinburgh or Glasgow and only 90 minutes from Inverness. Plenty to do here with walking, fishing, sandy beaches, breath-taking sunsets, and seal spotting . Fabulous gardens (Inverewe and Attadale), museums and nature reserves.

Rooms (per person per night incl. breakfast)

1 King Size (5') Suite	(en suite)	£125
1 Super King (6') Suite	(en suite)	£125
1 Emperor (7') Suite	(en suite)	£125
Single Occupancy		£170- £190

Meals

Dinner (4 courses)	£45
(By prior arrangement)	

Opening Times

Mid-March to October.
Christmas Opening for an exclusive group.

Payment Options

Facilities & Services

The Property

Cardross House is magnificent! For anyone with an interest in historic buildings this is an absolute must. Built in 1598 as a Tower House with later additions, it occupies a commanding position on rising ground above the River Forth with magnificent views in all directions.

On arrival at Cardross House you drive through beautiful parkland to be welcomed first by the family dogs and then by Nicola into what is a wonderful blend of friendly informality and elegant formality - comfy chairs covered with blankets in the outer hall and family portraits covering the walls of the main hall and grand staircase. The house has a particularly fine formal drawing room and dining room both beautifully decorated and furnished with fine antiques; however guests will be served breakfast and dinner in the less formal atmosphere of a delightful small Georgian panelled dining room and be entertained in the evening in the charming library in front of a roaring fire.

The bedrooms are spacious, beautifully decorated and furnished and have wonderful views over the garden. The main bedroom has an en suite bathroom and a small open tower room, with dressing table and stool, leading off it, whilst the second bedroom has a private bathroom.

The Hosts

Archie and Nicola Orr Ewing are a delightful, charming and relaxed couple with a wide range of interests from fishing and shooting to music, art and gardening. They know exactly how to put their guests at ease and ensure their stay is a never to be forgotten experience and are keen to share the glories of this stunning area.

The Location

Easy access from Edinburgh, Glasgow and Perth make this is an ideal location. Both east and west coast attractions are within range as are Loch Lomond and Trossachs National Park. There are wonderful castles at Stirling and Doune, historic Bannockburn and the Wallace Monument to visit, and magnificent mountains to climb.

Sir Archie & Lady Orr Ewing
Cardross
Port of Menteith
Kippen, By Stirling
Stirlingshire FK8 3JY
Tel: 01877 385223
stay@cardrossestate.com
www.cardrossestate.com   9931

Finding Us

A811 from Stirling. Take B8034 signposted to Port of Menteith. 2 miles on cross River Forth. Cardross drive 150yds on RIGHT (Yellow Lodge). If coming from Port of Menteith on B8034 go through Dykehead hamlet and Cardross drive is 100yds on LEFT

Rooms (per person per night incl. breakfast)

1 Twin (2 x 3′6″) Room (en suite)		£60
1 Twin (2 x 3′) Room (private)		£55
Single Supplement		£15

10% discount for 3 nights or more

Meals

Dinner – by prior arrangement   £35

Opening Times

Closed Christmas & New Year

Payment Options

Facilities & Services

DISCOVER WALES

Wales is rich in culture and traditions - having its own language and cultural events famous throughout the world.

Wherever you travel in Wales you will find friendly faces, fine food and things to see and do in abundance. And, you will find Wolsey Lodges in some of the most beautiful areas from the spectacular Welsh Marches; to the coastal delights of Pembrokeshire and Cardigan Bay; the majesty of the Snowdonia National Park and the North Wales borderlands.

From top: Whitesands Bay, Pembrokeshire; Dolbadarn Castle, Gwynedd; Cardiff.

Keith & Valerie Harber
Coedllys Country House,
Llangynin, St Clears,
Carmarthenshire SA33 4JY
Tel: 01994 231455
Fax: 01994 231441
coedllys@btinternet.com
www.coedllyscountryhouse.co.uk 6992

The Property

An idyllic, rural scene greets you at this old farmhouse and animal sanctuary with duck and peafowl ambling across the courtyard and a riot of colourful annuals and evergreens cascading from tubs and hanging baskets. Nestled in eleven acres of rolling fields and woodlands, it offers stunning views of the surrounding countryside.

A sense of sanctuary prevails in every sense at this multi award winning accommodation. Warm and welcoming receptions rooms are beautifully and classically decorated. The sitting room and bedrooms overlook rolling countryside and beautiful woodland, cottage gardens and ponds. Traditional Laura Ashley wallpapers, fabrics and soft furnishings enhance the relaxed, intimate and tranquil atmosphere. All rooms have heavenly, comfortable, welcoming and indulgent antique beds, with Hungarian goose down duvets and pillows and the very best of crisp linens. Wi-Fi, squishy sofas, power showers, slippers, fruit, flowers, Molton Brown products and pamper baskets leave guest in no doubt that they are being completely and utterly spoilt!.

The Hosts

Valerie and Keith offer nothing but the very best; the ultimate in comfort. their guests, return time and again to enjoy their warm hospitality. They both retired from the Police, where they worked for many years in the Royalty Protection Branch. The couple run an animal sanctuary with rescued donkeys, ponies, sheep, Alpaca, miniature Shetland pony, chickens, ducks and pea foul. Guests love the animals and the animals love the guests!

The Location

Carmarthenshire and Pembrokeshire have stunning beaches and breathtaking coastal walks. The National Botanical Gardens of Wales and Aberglasney gardens are close by, as are many National Trust properties and Laugharne, home of Dylan Thomas.

Finding Us

A40 to St. Clears roundabout. Take third exit to traffic lights. Turn left at lights. Approximately 100 yards on, road forks to right (signed Llangynin). Turn right here. Continue for 3 miles to Llangrynin, immediately after 30mph signs, turn left, then turn left after approximately 300 yards for Coedllys.

Rooms (per person per night incl. breakfast)

2 King Size (5') Rooms (en suite)	**£45-£50**
1 Twin (2 x 3') Room (en suite)	**£45-£50**
Single occupancy	**£80**

Meals

Light Supper	**£12**
(home made soup & sandwiches)	

Opening Times

Closed Christmas

Payment Options

Facilities & Services

Graham and Johanna Jackson
Maesmor Hall,
Maerdy, Corwen, Conwy LL21 0NS
Tel: 01490 460411
Fax: 01490 460441
maesmorhall@aol.com
www.maesmor.com   6991

Finding Us
From LLangollen, travelling west on A5 head
for Corwen. After Corwen cross River Dee.
Go straight through two sets of traffic lights
still on A5. After 2 miles turn left opposite
The Goat Pub, over narrow river bridge and
gates are in front of you.

The Property
Maesmor Hall is the perfect base from which to explore
North Wales, to be as active or as relaxed as you choose, to
be a culture vulture or follow a quest into the rich historical
past - whilst having superb comfort to come 'home' to.

Documented from the early 1200s, its ancient heritage sits
comfortably with all the modern luxuries one could wish
for, including an indoor heated swimming pool, with sauna,
overlooking the river.

The country house ambience is enhanced with antique and
new furniture. Paintings in the drawing room, dining room
and oak panelled hall make for a cosy welcome on a
winter's day with the fire blazing. Beautiful and spacious
en suite bedrooms, brimming with every comfort, have
lovely garden views.

Parkland and woodland, carpeted with early snowdrops,
border 11 acres of sweeping lawns, croquet lawn, tennis
court, summerhouse, a stretch of river and a water garden.

The Hosts
Johanna has a natural flair for welcoming and entertaining
guests and for many years ran her own restaurant, so
providing delicious food to discerning guests is second
nature. Both she and Graham enjoy country life, travel
and enjoy the rich cultural diversity of the area.

The Location
Every type of rugged outdoor pursuit (and those of a more
gentle nature) is available - from walking to mountaineering;
viewing waterfalls to whitewater rafting; golf, lake sailing
and windsurfing. The Llangollen Eisteddfod; hot air balloon
festivals, open air theatre, concerts; canal or narrow gauge
railway journeys; Anglesey, Snowdonia, Chester,
Shrewsbury, Caernarfon, Betws-y-Coed and Portmeirion
Village are just some of the region's varied attractions.

Rooms (per person per night incl. breakfast)

1 Super King (6') Room (en suite) **£45-£50**

I King Size (5'6") Room (en suite) **£45-£50**

Single Supplement   **£15**

Meals
Dinner   **£35**
(By prior arrangement)

Opening Times
Closed Christmas & New Year

Payment Options

Facilities & Services

Debbie Loughborough
Bryn Derwen
34 Abbey Road, Llandudno,
Conwy LL30 2EE
Tel: 01492 876804
brynderwen34@btinternet.com
www.bryn-derwen.co.uk   6972

Finding Us

Exit A55 signed Llandudno, join A470 towards Llandudno. On approach to town take 3rd at Links Hotel roundabout, over next roundabout to promenade. At mini roundabout turn left along seafront, proceed to Cenotaph, then turn left and go straight over roundabout. At next roundabout go straight over then take 2nd right on to York Road, Bryn Derwen is directly in front of you.

The Property

This elegant, substantial villa, built in 1878 as a holiday home for a wealthy Victorian businessman, has been sympathetically converted, into a superb guest house, retaining key original features including rare stained glass windows. It offers spacious and luxurious accommodation within walking distance of all the attractions in Llandudno, 'Queen of the Welsh Resorts'.

Guests relax in the comfortable and spacious lounge, or the lovely walled garden, over welcome drinks and home made Welsh cakes on arrival. An ornate pitch pine staircase ascends to the generously proportioned bedrooms, each with en suite shower/bathroom and individually furnished with the addition of sumptuous towels and bathrobes, indulgent toiletries and a generous hospitality tray.

Freshly cooked breakfasts are served at separate tables in the dining room. A traditional Welsh cooked option is available using locally sourced bacon and sausages with home made preserves and speciality teas on offer. Guests wanting a lighter start to the day can indulge in kippers.

The Hosts

Debbie and Steve relocated from Yorkshire with their two daughters ten years ago, leaving management positions in banking, for a new life in hospitality. Judging by their reviews and accolades they are naturals! Steve is in a male voice choir and they both enjoy varying sporting activities to keep fit. Nothing is too much trouble for their guests and they are pleased to advise and book a range of restaurants and hostelries and other activities for guests.

The Location

The largest seaside resort in Wales, with its original pier, bandstand and beautiful beaches, Llandudno has a plethora of cultural and sporting amenities. The Great Orme conservation area, rich in historic features; Lewis Carroll's links to the area; a Bronze Age copper mine; numerous National Trust properties, castles and gardens can all be explored in this popular town.

AA
★★★★★
Guest House

Rooms (per person per night incl. breakfast)

6 Double (4'6") Rooms (en suite)	**£40-£51**
1 Family Double (4'6") &	**£44-£47**
1 Single (3') Room (en suite)	
2 Twin (2 x 3') Room (en suite)	**£40-£47**

Meals

Breakfast only

Opening Times

Closed Mid December to Mid January

Payment Options

Facilities & Services

The Property

Overlooking the Vale of Clwyd, the gardens surrounding Firgrove are a blend of exotic, colourful and inspired planting that will delight gardening enthusiasts and non-gardeners alike. The house itself is a Grade II listed Georgian gem and home since the mid 1980's to your hosts Philip and Anna Meadway.

The graciousness of a bygone era overlays brightly decorated rooms furnished with antiques, collectibles, art and photographs whilst from every window there are views of the garden and countryside beyond. One guest room is in the main house and the second – the cottage suite – has a separate entrance and a sitting room with a fire. Everything you could wish for has been thought of right down to the home made cake on your arrival.

Dining here is a particular pleasure with a menu offering local, seasonal Welsh produce all cooked to perfection and enjoyed in a relaxed and exceptionally friendly atmosphere. Breakfast features a medley of fresh fruit, cereals, yogurt, ham and cheese as well as a traditional cooked option which, together with Philip and Anna's intimate knowledge of the best places to visit, really will set you up for the day ahead.

The Hosts

Philip, a retired professional runs Firgrove with Anna who had retired several years before from her family's business in Ruthin. Gardening intensively and looking after their many visitors, they enjoy regular forays to France to hunt for new delicacies for their guests.

The Location

Perfectly located in North Wales for walking, exploring, bird watching, cycling and shopping there is the Snowdonia National Park, Ruthin and its Craft Centre, Llangollen with its festivals and the nearby awe-inspiring Pont Cysyllte aquaduct, Roman Chester and its famous 'Rows', Llandudno and Llandegla Forest.

Anna & Philip Meadway
Firgrove
Llanfwrog
Ruthin
Denbighshire LL15 2LL
Tel: 01824 702677 or 07710 251606
meadway@firgrovecountryhouse.co.uk
www.firgrovecountryhouse.co.uk 6976

Finding Us

Exit Ruthin on A494 to Bala. At mini roundabout go straight on B5105 signed 'Cerrig y Drudion'. Pass church on right and Ye Olde Cross Keys on left. Remain on road travelling ¼ mile driving uphill. Firgrove is large house set above road on right with large pine trees on roadside.

Rooms (per person per night incl. breakfast)

2 Double (4'6") Rooms (en suite)	£45-£55
Single Supplement	£25

Meals

Dinner	£38

Opening Times

Usually closed November to February inclusive.

Payment Options

Facilities & Services

Katrina le Saux & Peter Cottee
Bryniau Golau,
Llangower, Bala, Gwynedd LL23 7BT
Tel: 01678 521782
katrinalesaux@hotmail.co.uk
www.bryniau-golau.co.uk 6985

Finding Us
From Bala, take B4391 towards LLangynog, follow road around until Bala Lake is visible on right. Turn right on B4403 to Llangower. Pass Bala Lake Hotel on left and after approximately ¼ mile Bryniau Golau is 2nd turning on the left. Go up the tarmac road, over cattle grid and Bryniau Golau is the first house on the right.

The Property
Bryniau Golau is a haven of peace and tranquillity offering stunning views across Bala Lake to the Arenig mountains beyond. The pretty town of Bala is within walking distance; dating from the 14th century it offers a warm Welsh welcome.

The house is Victorian and has been tastefully refurbished with the help of an interior designer. The comfortable sitting room, solely for guests use, has a log fire and an honesty bar; the dining room has a Bechstein piano which musicians are welcome to use. The garden has a terraced area, perfect for relaxing and watching the sunset.

The three spacious bedrooms, all recently re-decorated, offer every comfort with spa baths, power showers and under-floor heating in the en suite bathrooms, goose down duvets, electric blankets and homemade biscuits. Two bedrooms have antique four poster beds, the third a super king bed which may split into two singles.

The food is superb. Peter is a talented cook and evening meals are available on Fridays and Sundays. Special diets are catered for. Bryniau Golau holds a drinks licence and there is an excellent wine list available. All food is homemade or locally sourced; bread, granola, preserves (including award winning marmalade) and honey from the hives make the breakfasts memorable occasions.

The Hosts
Katrina and Peter have great energy and enthusiasm and are dedicated to ensuring their guests have a wonderful stay. Nothing is too much trouble and they are keen to share their love and knowledge of this area. Katrina is from a nursing/midwifery background and Peter has a corporate background.

The Location
Bryniau Golau is within Snowdonia National Park, in an area of breathtaking beauty, enhanced by castles and gardens, historic town and cities. There is easy access for uncrowded shorelines and opportunities for canoeing, sailing, fishing, guided walks and white water rafting for the more adventurous.

Rooms (per person per night incl. breakfast)

1 Super King (6')/ Twin Room (en suite)	£60
1 King Size (5') Four Poster Room (en suite)	£60
1 King Size (5') Four Poster Room (en suite)	£55
Single Occupancy	£75

Meals

Supper	£25
Dinner	£30

(Meals available Friday & Sunday)

Opening Times
Closed Christmas

Payment Options

Facilities & Services

Lady Hallinan
Cotham Lodge
West Street
Newport
Pembrokeshire SA42 0TD
Tel: 01239 820341
hallinan.cotham@btinternet.com   **6997**

Finding Us

On the A487 Cardigan to Fishguard road. From Cardigan go through the village, the house is on the right next to the Memorial Hall with entrance gates on the corner. From Fishguard, the house is on the left bend of the hill going down to Newport.

The Property

This Grade II listed, period dower house built in 1787, is set in delightful grounds overlooking the sea.

Across a small courtyard is a cottage, built at the same time, in the traditional Pembrokeshire manner in stone and flint. It has a 'chimney fawr' (a large fire hearth incorporating a bread oven and water boiler). The cottage has been renovated to a high standard with two bedrooms and bathroom and a downstairs shower room. It has its own sitting room. In the house there is a spacious double room with its own bathroom.

The Host

Lady Hallinan welcomes people to this traditional Welsh family home as if they were house guests. For guests who would wish to eat out on occasion there are good restaurants and public houses in the village, no need to take a car.

The Location

The small ancient borough of Trefdraeth (Newport) with its own Norman Castle is in the Pembrokeshire National Park and easily accessible. It is on the coastal walk, which stretches both north and south with marvellous seascape walking. Lady Hallinan is happy to advise guests on the many attractions of the area. It is an ideal centre for ornithologists, for exploring the unspoilt countryside, the mountains and seashores of both Cardiganshire and Pembrokeshire. St. David's Cathedral, the National Trust Colby Gardens, ancient castles, monuments and many artists and craft galleries are nearby. It is convenient for the Fishguard/Rosslare ferry and the Paddington/Fishguard train.

Rooms (per person per night incl. breakfast)

2 Double (4' 6") Rooms	**£45**
(1 en suite / 1 private)	
1 Twin (2 x 3') Room (private)	**£45**

Meals

Dinner	**£25**

Opening Times

Closed Christmas & New Year

Payment Options

Facilities & Services

The Property

If you're looking for a place to stay that has the 'wow' factor then this is it. Beautiful house, stunning location, friendliest hostess and fabulous food combine to ensure you will want to return again and again. Crug-Glas is a tastefully restored Georgian house set in 600 acres of farmland with glorious views in every direction and beautiful gardens to relax in.

There is a wonderful blend of antique and modern furnishings throughout and the bedrooms and bathrooms are sumptuous with huge beds, crisp bed linen and soft bathrobes. There is a recently renovated 'honeymoon suite' on the top floor with beautiful bedroom, sitting room and bathroom with spa bath.

Janet is an amazing cook whose restaurant at Crug-Glas has won significant acclaim. She prepares her menus each day according to what fresh meat, fish or vegetables have been delivered and guests make their choice from a wonderful selection of starters, main courses and puddings and Janet then produces the most wonderful dinners that would tempt the most jaded palate. Crug-Glas is fully licensed and there is an 'honesty bar' in the sitting room so guests can relax over a drink after dinner.

The Hosts

Janet is the most friendly hostess with a ready smile and an instinct for knowing exactly how to spoil her guests. Whilst her husband is busy running the farm Janet is happy to entertain interested guests with the history of the farm which dates back to the 13th century.

The Location

St Davids peninsula is a stunning area with walks along coastal paths and glorious beaches. The tiny St Davids Cathedral is not to be missed and there are Pembroke and Picton Castles to visit along with Skomer and Ramsey Islands for their wildlife and fascinating woollen mills at Tregwynt and Middle Mill.

Janet Evans
Crug-Glas, Near Abereiddy, Solva,
Haverfordwest, Pembrokeshire SA62 6XX
Tel: 01348 831302
janet@crugglas.plus.com
www.crug-glas.co.uk   6983

Finding Us

Situated on the A487 St Davids to Fishguard approx 3½ miles outside of St Davids, pass through village of Carnhedryn, first left half a mile after the village.

Rooms   (per person per night incl. breakfast)

2 King Size (5') Rooms (en suite)	**£70**
1 Super King (6')/Twin Room (en suite)	**£75**
1 Emperor (7') Four Poster Room (en suite)	**£75**
1 King Size (5') Suite (en suite)	**£85**
Coach House 1 Super King (6') (en suite)	**£85**
Long House 1 Super King (6')/Twin (en suite)	**£85**

Meals

Dinner (3 courses)	**from £20**

Opening Times

Closed Christmas

Payment Options

Facilities & Services

The Property

Cresselly House is one of Pembrokeshire's finest houses and is occasionally opened for public tours. Allen family ancestors of the current owner built this gorgeous classic Georgian house in 1769. Overlooking the Cleddau Estuary it is set in 16 acres of elegant grounds and woodlands that guests can enjoy. This is a spectacular member of the Wolsey Lodge Welsh portfolio.

Behind the almost austere facade lies a home of great warmth and charm. After entering the grand hall, decorated with portraits of Allen ancestors and an abundance of fox hunting mementos from the past, guests will be welcomed in the beautiful drawing room, which they can also use during their stay. Up the grand staircase there are very spacious guest bedrooms and enormous bathrooms with separate shower cubicles and capacious baths. Each has been recently restored and individually furnished in sumptuous classic style - with many of the family's lovely antiques - in keeping with the elegance of the property.

A delicious dinner, by arrangement, and hearty breakfasts are served in the formal dining room. The estate has its own free range hens and is currently re-establishing its two acre walled kitchen garden to provide additional fresh produce for guests to enjoy.

The Hosts

Running the estate and its numerous events, together with his keen interest in horseracing keep Hugh busy when he isn't welcoming his guests. Ros has her own catering company, and they both enjoy their involvement in the catering at Cresselly. The creamy scrambled eggs at breakfast are one of Hugh's specialities!

The Location

Ideally positioned for visiting the beautiful Pembrokeshire Coast National Park and the lovely town of Tenby, this area is steeped in National Trust sites. Lovely woodlands, country walks, castles and gardens to visit, boat trips and more are within easy reach. A simply wonderful place to explore all that Pembrokeshire has to offer.

Hugh Harrison-Allen & Ros Beck
Cresselly House
Cresselly, Pembrokeshire SA68 0SP
Tel: 01646 651992
info@cresselly.com
www.cresselly.com   6970

Finding Us

Cresselly lies just east of A4075 which can be reached from the road to Haverfordwest (A40). As you come into Cresselly village, going slightly uphill, look for high stone garden wall on right. Shortly after it ends, take small side road signed Cresswell Quay and just down on right is main entrance drive to the house. Please note gates are narrow so you should swing wide.

Rooms (per person per night incl. breakfast)

1 Super King (6') Room	(en suite)	**£55-£75**
1 King Size (5') Room	(en suite)	**£55-£75**
1 King Size (5') Four Poster Room (en suite)		**£55-£75**
1 Twin (2 x 3') Room	(en suite)	**£55-£75**
1 Single (1 x 3') Room	(private)	**£85**

Meals

Supper (2 Courses)	**£28**
Dinner (3 Courses)	**£38**
(Both by prior arrangement)	

Opening Times

Open all year

Payment Options

Facilities & Services

Warwick & Christina Jackson
Glangrwyney Court
Crickhowell, Powys NP8 1ES
Tel: 01873 811288
info@glancourt.co.uk
www.glancourt.co.uk　　　　6969

Finding Us
Located just off A40 to Brecon. When approaching via Abergavenny follow signs "A40 Brecon" passing Nevill Hall Hospital on left. Continue along road for approximately 3 miles. You will see "POWYS" County change sign on left and the drive is next on right, with signs reading "Glangrwyney Court" opposite and a little Lodge/Cottage at the entrance.

Rooms (per person per night incl. breakfast)

2 Double (4'6") Rooms (en suite)	**£67.50**
5 King Size (5') Rooms (en suite)	**£72.50**
1 Super King (6')/Twin (en suite)	**£67.50**
1 Super King (6')/Twin (private)	**£57.50**

Meals
Breakfast only

Opening Times
Open all year

Payment Options

Facilities & Services

The Property
A superb Grade II listed country house estate where Wolsey Lodges meets luxury boutique hotel. Set in four acres of inspirational gardens within 33 acres of parkland, this late 18th century house puts the 'treat' into 'retreat'. With luxury accommodation and service very much 21st century, a warm welcome is assured here.

The house itself is elegantly decorated in classic style. The graceful drawing room has deep sofas around a wood-burning stove and guests can help themselves to drinks from the honesty bar. The nine bedrooms furnished with antiques and interesting objects, are exceptional in terms of comfort and décor. Eight are en suite and one has a private bathroom with whirlpool bath. In line with the stylish elegance of the public rooms, bedrooms provide every comfort including television, DVD player, hospitality tray, bathrobes and luxury toiletries. Croquet, tennis and boules can be played here.

Tea and a biscuit tray is available on arrival and evening meals can be arranged for groups of six or more. Delicious breakfasts (including a Full Welsh with locally sourced produce) are served in the charming dining room with lovely views of the garden.

The Hosts
Warwick and Christina along with their daughters Rachel and Rebecca love sharing their superb family home with guests. Nothing is too much trouble and they will provide packed lunches, book tables at local restaurants, arrange transport and be pleased to advise on the many fabulous local walks and cycle routes.

The Location
Close to the Brecon Beacons National Park and Waterfall Country with mountain trails, horse riding, limestone caves, forests, fishing at Wye Foundation, castles, gold mines, museums, fairs, festivals, a historic canal as well as some charming, characterful towns such as Abergavenny and Monmouth. Foodies will love the Michelin-starred restaurants and farmers' markets and there is something here to appeal to all ages.

Paul Gerrard
The Old Vicarage
Norton, Presteigne
Radnorshire, Powys LD8 2EN
Tel: 01544 260038
paul@nortonoldvic.co.uk   **6988**
www.oldvicarage-nortonrads.co.uk

Finding Us

The Old Vicarage is at Norton on the B4355, between Presteigne and Knighton. From Presteigne, the house is the first drive on the right after the church. Full directions on www.oldvicarage-nortonrads.co.uk

The Property

The spectacular Welsh Marches and Powys countryside are the perfect backdrop for The Old Vicarage, a Gothic style house designed by Sir George Gilbert Scott in the 1860s on the bailey of a Norman castle and now a perfect luxury bed and breakfast retreat. Every room inside The Old Vicarage is testament to your host Paul's attention to detail, from the period fixtures such as the restored servants' bells, exquisite gas, oil and electric light fittings, richly coloured wallpaper and fabrics, to the lovingly collected Victorian furniture.

The guest bedrooms are each uniquely furnished with antiques offering a complete haven for comfort and relaxation. Both the Green Price room and the Gilbert Scott room have king size double beds whilst the Burlinson room has a super king size four poster bed. Outside, the landscaped gardens were designed by Chelsea award winner Paul Cooper and guests can enjoy exploring the paths, walkways, follies, pond and waterfall that are to be found in this delightful and tranquil garden with the stunning countryside of Wales all around.

The Hosts

Paul Gerrard is your relaxed, friendly and welcoming host for your stay at The Old Vicarage in Presteigne and is a professional chef who delights in providing food sourced from the local Powys area. A fund of knowledge about all things Victorian, Paul is always keen to share his love and knowledge of Victorian architecture with his guests.

The Location

The Old Vicarage is on the edge of the village of Norton, near Presteigne in Powys. Named by Country Life as one of the top ten places to live, Presteigne is a former assize and county town offering an award winning museum and a renowned music festival every August. The house is just a short drive from the many attractions of Wales offering something for all guests including inspiring walks, Michelin starred restaurants and wonderful drives through the Cambrian Mountains to Cardigan Bay.

Rooms (per person per night incl. breakfast)

2 King Size (5') Rooms (en suite)	**£49.50-£56**
1 Super King Four Poster (6') / Twin Room (en suite)	**£49.50-£56**
Single Occupancy	**£78**

Meals

Dinner	**£34.95**

Opening Times

Open all year

Payment Options

Facilities & Services

EXPLORE FRANCE

France is a land of contrasts. Rich culture mingles with heritage and stunning scenery wherever you turn. Snowy alpine peaks, rich and verdant countryside and chic cities offer a wealth of experiences for travellers.

A 'taste of home with a different twist' is how we would describe this handful of exclusive Lodges in that they offer all the welcome and hospitality so synonymous with Wolsey Lodges, combined with the thrill and excitement of uncovering the real charm of th beautiful locations.

Top: Rando Chaine des Pays; below right: Chatanvuax

The Property

South of Caen in the wooded Suisse Normande region, lies the pretty village of Culey le Patry. Chateau La Cour is the largest and oldest property hereabouts, dating back to the 13th century, its façade and interior richly evoking links with Richard the Lionheart.

Beautiful wood panelling, traditional tiled floors and elegant double doors decorated with cast iron work, complement the impressive stone staircase leading to three large bedrooms: 'Papillon' with its sumptuous king size double bed, sofa and private stairs leading to an en suite bathroom; the kind sized double or twin bedded 'Fleur de Lys' with Lloyd Loom chairs, writing desk and stunning en suite with king size bath; and the double 'Rosa' with en suite and window seat from which you can gaze endlessly at the Normandy landscape. Secure parking is available.

Candlelit four course dinners and informal three course suppers feature locally sourced ingredients with vegetables, herbs and fruits from the lovingly tended potager and wild mushrooms foraged from the forest; and a truly splendid gourmet Continental breakfast prove that the heart of French living is good food and wine. Vegetarians are very welcome!

The Hosts

David and Lesley have created a piece of paradise. They enjoy meeting people and guests relish the real taste of relaxed Normandy life. Their special interest is food. They take great care in the sourcing of ingredients and the preparation and presentation of the dishes they serve.

The Location

The area offers a range of outdoor pursuits, including golf and walking and is an excellent base for visiting sophisticated Honfleur, Deauville, Bayeux and the D-Day Landing Beaches. Mont St Michel and Monet's garden are also easily accessible.

David and Lesley Craven
Chateau La Cour,
14220 Culey le Patry,
Normandy, France
Tel: 00 33 (0) 2 31 79 19 37
info@chateaulacour.com
www.chateaulacour.com   4394

Finding Us

From Caen or from the south, travel on the D562. At Pont de la Mousse, 5kms south of Thury Harcourt, take D133 for Culey le Patry over the river Orne. Turn left onto D166, then second right onto D211. La Cour is on right, on the approach to village, just after first minor road to the right.

Rooms   (per person per night incl. breakfast)

2 King Size (5') Rooms (en suite)	€75
1 King Size (5')/Twin Room (en suite)	€75
Single Supplement	€25

Meals

Supper 3 courses (incl. wine)	€36
Dinner 4 courses (incl. wine)	€50
(Both by prior arrangement)	

Opening Times

Open March to October

Payment Options

Facilities & Services

Comte and Comtesse de Vanssay
Chateau de la Barre, Conflans sur
Anille, Sarthe F-72120, France
Tel: 00 33 (0) 2 43 35 00 17
info@chateaudelabarre.com
www.chateaudelabarre.com   4393

Finding Us
Take the 'La Ferte Bernard' exit from motorway
A11 (Paris to Le Mans-Nantes). Follow D1 through
Vibraye & Berfay. La Barre is 5.5km after Berfay,
600m on your right, after the turn down towards
Conflans which you do not take. Coming from
Calais via Rouen, take A28 and exit after Le Mans
East, then follow N157 past St. Calais, to the D1 for
about 2km. Turn left into La Barre Drive.

The Property
Experience the gracious hospitality of French aristocracy
as guests of Count and Countess de Vanssay, at Château
de La Barre, home to their family for more than 610 years.
Secluded in the midst of a 100 acre private park with
fragrant gardens, XVIth century fortifications, and a family
chapel, this elegant Château mixes rare antiques, fine
paintings and vibrant designer fabrics throughout, creating a
chic environment full of warmth and understated luxury.

Seven en suite rooms and suites offer exquisite linens and
precious furniture without compromising on contemporary
comforts.

Your Hosts
Twice a week, Guy and Marnie host a 'Grand Siècle'
dinner in their ornate 18th century reception rooms. On
other nights, a light supper can be laid out in the majestic
XIVth century 'pièce à feu', where a game of billiards can
be enjoyed under the watchful eyes of the Fox Terrier, the
Weimaraner and Kakou the macaw parrot.

The Location
Less than 2 hours from Paris and Normandy, this is the
perfect place from which to discover the famous Loire
Valley castles, and also explore the untouched countryside
of the little Loir Valley with its many romantic gardens, XIIth
century Romanesque churches, wineries, colourful farmers
markets and gourmet restaurants.

Sport lovers can enjoy a riding school and three golf courses
nearby and the use of complimentary bicycles on site. On
certain dates, it is even possible to drive a race car around
the Le Mans track!

In the summer, don't miss the classical concerts and the
magical Light show in the medieval Plantagenet City of Le
Mans.

Rooms (per person per night incl. breakfast)
3 Super King (6') Rooms   €175-€235
(en suite)
2 King Size (5') Rooms   €148-€175
(en suite)
1 Twin (2 x 3'6") Room (en suite)   €175
1 Single (3'6") Room   (en suite)   €170
Minimum stay 2 nights, special discounts on
3 nights or more

Meals
Supper (excl. Wine)   €65
Dinner (served twice a week)   €140
(Grand Dining Room, champagne, wine,
coffee and brandy included).
(Both upon prior reservation only)

Opening Times
Closed 11 January to 11 March

Payment Options

Facilities & Services

The Property

Chateau de Villette offers guests a very special, peaceful and tranquil haven in a remote country setting amongst the Morvan Hills. Formerly occupied by French aristocracy and recently renovated, the chateau has been sumptuously redecorated with meticulous attention paid to the three large guest rooms which are furnished with the finest furniture and linen, have their own private bathrooms and views across the park.

The 500 acre estate surrounding the chateau has been carefully cultivated using environmentally friendly farming and conservation practices to provide stunning scenic contrasts – centuries old parkland, formal terraces, beautiful woodland and crystal clear streams merge together to create an idyllic setting to the perfect relaxing break. Chateau de Villette organises unique driven game shooting on wild partridge, pheasant and wild boar.

Food is sourced locally to ensure guests experience the very best of this region's outstanding culinary delights and fine wines. A minimum of twenty four hours notice is required for dinner.

The Hosts

Coen and Catherine Stork share a love of this beautiful area of Burgundy and they extend a very natural, warm and enthusiastic welcome to guests that discover the very special retreat they have created at the Chateau de Villette. The hosts have an in-depth knowledge of the local area and delight in sharing this with guests.

The Location

It would be hard to visit this area without visiting the local vineyards and there is an abundance to choose from. Alongside this there are local antique markets to explore, tennis and walking and, by going slightly further afield, guests can take day trips to Roman churches and private chateaux not normally open to the public.

Mr & Mrs Coen Stork
Chateau de Villette
58170 Poil, Burgundy, France
Tel: 00 33 (0)3 86 30 09 13
chateaudevillette@icloud.com
www.chateaudevillette.eu   4385

Finding Us

On the N81, between Autun and Luzy. 18km from Autun, turn right onto the D192 for Poil. Drive through the tiny village of Poil and 2km after leaving the village, turn left for 'Villette'.

Rooms (per person per night incl. breakfast)

2 Super King (6') Suites (en suite)	**€115**
1 Super King (6') Four Poster Suite (en suite)	**€135**
1 King Size (5') Room (en suite)	**€100**
1 Twin (2 x 3') Room (en suite)	**€100**

Meals

Dinner	**€55**
(Wed & Sat only - by prior arrangement)	
Supper	**€24**
(e.g Cheese Platter)	

Opening Times

Open all year

Payment Options

Facilities & Services

Sacha de Frisching
Domaine de la Freynelle
33420 Espiet
St Emilion
France
Tel: 00 33 (0) 5 57 24 97 42
sachitza@yahoo.com
www.brunchcaviar.com   4381

Finding Us
Detailed directions available on request.

Rooms
(per person per night incl. breakfast)

1 King Size (5') Apartment (en suite)	€60
1 King Size (5') Suite (en suite)	€65
1 Twin Room (2 x 3') (en suite)	€50

Meals

Supper   (3 courses inc. Wine)   €35

Caviar tastings

(Both by prior arrangement)

Opening Times
Open May - September

Payment Options

Facilities & Services

The Property
On the outskirts of Espiet and deceptively discreet from
the road, the manor house was built in 1773 and its
restoration has been a true labour of love for the owner. It
is set in seven hectares of grounds, of which two acres are
beautifully landscaped gardens with ancient cedars and
a sea of pink and white roses. It boasts a heated outdoor
pool, tennis court, par 3 golf hole, medieval vegetable
garden and, of course, a petanque court!

Meals are a pleasure, whether around the carved walnut
dining table or on the stunning terrace. Spacious,airy rooms
with high ceilings and caramel tones are decorated with
antique bric a brac.

There are two 'fin du siecle' style guest bedrooms, one a
four poster, the other a twin in the main house. The suite
has its own fitness area. There is also an apartment offering
usual Wolsey Lodges hospitality adjacent to the house.

The Host
Hostess Sacha de Frisching is Swiss by birth, with a Croatian
mother but educated in England and France. She has lived
in Europe, South America and Cuba and is fluent in five
languages. Formerly a journalist, Sacha de Frisching is also a
children's writer and author of a cookbook 'Brunch Caviar'.
Her ebullient manner, endless energy and enthusiasm for
her home and gardens make her the perfect hostess. She
likes to promote locally farmed sturgeon roe, which can be
sampled and is served by prior arrangement.

The Location
Located in the relatively undiscovered Aquitaine region
in south west France, stretching from the Dordogne to
Bordeaux. Close to St Emilion, the 'mecca' for lovers of
Bordeaux wines, it is the perfect base. Flea markets, food
and wine markets and cultural festivals abound, as do lakes
and rivers offering water sports and cruises.

Mr Francis Van der Elst
Chateau de Moulin le Comte
44 rue Principale
Moulin-le-Comte
F-62120 Aire-sur-la-Lys
France
Tel: 00 33 (0) 6 24 21 08 91 or
    00 33 (0) 3 21 88 48 38
info@chateaudemoulinlecomte.com **4380**
www.chateaudemoulinlecomte.com

The Property

This elegant 19th century luxury chambres d'hôte mansion has been beautifully restored with careful attention to its original character and offers the perfect stopover or a base for a relaxed break in this beautiful area, just 45 minutes from Calais.

This chateau is situated on the outskirts of historic Aire-sur-la-Lys. Extensive gardens, with outside seating for guests to enjoy, are gradually being renovated and there is ample parking. Inside it is decorated in classic French style but the very spacious bedrooms have stylish contemporary touches and the en suite bathrooms are definitely 21st century! Large beds, quality linen, bathrobes, toiletries, television, WiFi, a hospitality tray and fresh flowers add a homely touch and one bedroom is on the ground floor.

There is a guest salon with a bar for aperitifs (or served on the terrace, weather permitting). Breakfasts plus delicious dinners (by prior arrangement) are served in the elegant dining room with separate tables (grouped together for larger parties).

The Hosts

Francis and Cedric, this very welcoming father and son team, are Flemish and speak no less than seven languages! Francis is the chef, who produces a fantastic, very reasonably priced five course table d'hôte dinner. Generous 'Continental Plus' breakfasts to set you up for the day include home-made preserves, a selection of breads, pain au chocolat, cereals, eggs, cheese and cold meats.

The Location

For travellers, the Chateau is very handy for the AutoRoute but the Pas de Calais has a wealth of activities for those who can linger longer. Museums, galleries, monuments, markets, and shops abound, and outdoor enthusiasts can enjoy riding, fishing, golf, cycling and walking. The nearby Marais area offers a great family day out and foodies are spoilt for choice.

Finding Us

If using a navigation system, please use : France, 62120 Aire-sur-la Lys, 44 rue Principale, (Moulin-le-Comte) as there are 2 streets named Rue Principale in Aire-sur la Lys.

Rooms (per person per night incl. breakfast)

3 Superior Super King (6') / Twin Rooms (en suite)	**€59.50**
2 Super King (6')/Twin Rooms (en suite)	**€49.50**
Single Occupancy	**€79-€99**

Meals

Dinner (5 courses)	**€29**

Opening Times

Open all year

Payment Options

Facilities & Services

Australia
Accommodation Guide
The B&B Book

The B&B Book –The original Guide to wonderful accommodation.

Whatever the style, simple or deluxe, B&B or self contained you are treated as a special guest from the moment you arrive until the time you depart.

"A lifetime of memories."

Available from Book Shops in the UK or Mail Order
Inn Australia PO Box 330 Wahroonga NSW 2076
info@bbbook.com.au

www.BBBook.com.au
ISBN 978-0-9875756-0-9

For an unforgettable holiday count on RACV

RACV Resorts are located in some of Australia's best holiday destinations offering impressive facilities in picturesque locations:

- on the magnificent Mornington Peninsula in Victoria
- in the sunny Murray River region in Victoria
- on the stunning South Gippsland Bass Coast in Victoria
- on the popular Gold Coast in Queensland
- on the tranquil Sunshine Coast in Queensland
- on the spectacular Great Ocean Road in Victoria
- in historic Hobart in Tasmania

AUSTRALIA

Noosa
Gold Coast

Cobram

Torquay
Cape Schanck

Inverlo

Hobart

Discover more at
racv.com.au/resorts

RACV Resorts

Index

Look up Lodges by Country & County

● New member

● Weddings

● Exclusive use

(For more information please see page xi)

GIFT VOUCHERS

The perfect gift for special people

Share the secret of Wolsey Lodges with friends and family by giving them Wolsey Lodge Gift Vouchers and let them choose a Lodge of their choice from this year's brochure.

Available in denominations of £25 and £50 together with a copy of the current brochure with our compliments.

Ordering is simple - either visit our website www.wolseylodges.com and go to the secure secure on-line shop or call + 44 (0) 1473 822058 to pay by debit/credit card. Alternatively send a cheque to: Wolsey Lodges Ltd, 9 Market Place, Hadleigh, Ipswich, Suffolk IP7 5DL.

Terms and conditions apply for voucher redemptions. Vouchers can only be redeemed at Wolsey Lodges in the current brochure. To avoid disappointment please check that you hold the most up to date brochure and that you advise the Lodge both at the time of booking and when you arrive that you wish to redeem your vouchers.

From top: West Stow Hall, Suffolk and Roineabhal, Argyll – both Wolsey Lodges.